In the Footsteps of Jesus

Images of the Holy Land

In the Footsteps of Jesus

IMAGES OF THE HOLY LAND

PHOTOGRAPHS BY JOHN TELFORD

TEXT BY SUSAN EASTON BLACK

Covenant Communications, Inc.

Published by Covenant Communications, Inc.
American Fork, Utah

Printed in China
First Printing: October 1999

06 05 04 03 02 01 00 99   10 9 8 7 6 5 4 3 2 1

ISBN 1-57734-510-X

Library of Congress Cataloging-in-Publication Data

Black, Susan Easton,
     In the footsteps of Jesus : images of the Holy Land / photographs by John Telford ; text by Susan Easton Black.
          p.   cm.
     Includes bibliographical references.
     ISBN 1-57734-510-X
     1. Jesus Christ Biography. 2. Palestine Pictorial works.
     I. Telford, John,   II. Title.
     BT301.2.B53 1999
     225.9'1--dc21   99-36557
                              CIP

CONTENTS

Acknowledgments

For centuries the Bedouins have maintained a traditional nomadic lifestyle, living in tents and traveling the desert seeking fresh water and pastureland for their livestock.

(opposite page) The reconstructed arch and central area of the Hurva Synagogue (Hurva meaning "ruin"), originally built in 1701 for the Ashkenasi Jews, and later rebuilt in 1858. It was destroyed again in 1948 and except for the arch, has never been fully restored.

During the preparation of this book, we often asked ourselves, "Are we capable or worthy of presenting the life of Jesus in written and photographic format?" The many roadblocks we faced as we attempted to launch and then complete *In the Footsteps of Jesus* often led us to answer, "We are not capable and we are not worthy." Yet, knowing the compassion of Jesus, and that in our weakness we could find the strength of talents needed, we pressed forward. Our journey has not been easy, but the sincerity of our effort has not been compromised.

In what appeared at times a desert of discouragement, we found help from some of the greatest men and women who have devoted their lives to studying the life and teachings of the Lord Jesus Christ. Robert J. Matthews, a longtime friend and colleague in Brigham Young University's Religious Education, offered helpful historical and doctrinal observations for the social history. New Testament scholars Keith Meservy and Richard Draper meticulously pored over the text, searching for problem areas. We are most grateful to each of these scholars and friends for their willingness to share their years of faithful scholarship with us.

We also extend appreciation to General Education and Honors and the College of Fine Arts and Communication at Brigham Young University. Through generous grants from these colleges, the photographic journey in the Holy Land was made possible. Daniel Rona and the staff of Israel Revealed, along with Eric Toomey, were most helpful in providing accommodations and assistance with photography needs during our sojourns in the Holy Land.

The skill of secretaries Adele Marcum, Kristina Potter, Michelle Blauer, and Tori Gali was needed constantly through the various writing phases of *In the Footsteps of Jesus*. They approached each task with cheerfulness, and seemed to find joy in the opportunity of learning more about their Savior. When seeking a publisher, the enthusiasm of JoAnn Jolley, managing editor at Covenant Communications, Inc. was unmatched. We have not been disappointed with the fine caliber of the staff at Covenant and their willingness to work with us on this project.

To our eternal companions, who know best of our desire to share talent and testimony in word and picture, we express our love. Harvey and Valerie unwittingly sensed when encouragement was needed and confidence was lacking. Through them we have learned what it means to "Come unto Christ."

PHOTOGRAPHER'S PREFACE

Is this the land where Jesus walked? Are these the places he saw? Archaeologists and historians have identified numerous rulers who fought over, conquered, destroyed, and rebuilt this city and country, only to have it conquered, destroyed, and rebuilt again and again. I find myself wondering, "Did I walk today where Jesus walked?" My intellect tells me no. But my heart and soul want to believe I did, and my mind is willing to follow suit.

For five weeks, as I walked in paths and places spoken of in the scriptures, I wondered, "How does one grasp the magnitude and significance of these places in such a short time?" Seeing them at such a fast pace does not give me an adequate appreciation for the millennia of history passing by—5,000-year-old pyramids and temples, 9,000-year-old towns and battlefields. The names of prophets and kings and the places where they lived and died slide by as though I were on some amusement park ride. Frequently, I had to just stop and look around. "This is Jerusalem!" I'd say to myself. "You are in the Old City—the Holy City. Slow down until you can feel it. And then take the pictures."

I came to Jerusalem, to Israel, hoping to draw closer to Jesus, wanting to walk the paths where he had walked. Many times during my stay, I lamented not feeling his presence. The schedule was too hectic, or the noise or other distractions got in the way. While there were many times that I was touched, emotionally and spiritually, even to the point of tears, there was still something more I wanted—something unfulfilled.

A donkey atop the Mount of Olives. Jerusalem is in the background.

Grain fields near Bet Shemish (Samson country) form colorful patterns in the fertile valleys of Israel.

(opposite page) High on the Mount of Olives, overlooking the Old City of Jerusalem, is a grove of olive trees close to where many people believe the original Garden of Gethsemane was located.

While sitting on the Mount of Olives, and again while looking into the empty tomb in the peaceful garden, an answer came to me. It was similar to the answer given to Mary when she came looking for Jesus: "He is not here, [He] is risen" (Luke 24:6).

Simple, yet so profound. He is not found in the grotto of the Church of the Nativity, though Christians believe he was there. He is not found in any of the hundreds of churches that have been built on traditional sites of his ministry. There are many languages heard in those places, many rites witnessed, many fragrances wafting through the air carried with the chants, the singing, and the praying of many tongues seeking to find Jesus. But he is not there.

We find him today where he promised we would. We find him when we partake of the sacrament. We find him when we are gathered together in his name. We find him in his holy house. We find him in keeping his commandments.

Two thousand years have passed since the Mortal Messiah walked the paths and hillsides of Israel. Much has changed, yet much remains the same. The important question to ask is not whether I walked today where Jesus walked, but if I am walking today where Jesus would have me walk.

CHAPTER 1

THE ROAD TO BETHLEHEM

PHOTOGRAPHER'S NOTE - APRIL 29, 1998
BETHLEHEM

Where is the lowly stable? The Church of the Nativity, built in the sixth century, is a fortress-like structure with a small opening that forces all who visit to crouch or bend down to enter.

I arrived early in the morning in hopes of photographing the famous grotto in relative peace. As I entered the building I was alone, but tour buses soon arrived, bringing throngs of pilgrims from many countries. People rushed to the grotto to see a fourteen-point star marking the legendary birthplace of the Prince of Peace. Kneeling over the star, touching it, kissing it, dipping their fingers into a small basin of holy water in the middle of the star, they pushed and shoved to reach the spot. The crowd was pushing so hard behind me that I could scarcely bend over to set my camera and tripod on the marble floor. I waited for an opening in the crowd, quickly calculated the exposure, extended the flash, and fired.

Before the shutter closed, someone rushed in front of me to kneel at the star. Hands kept flashing into the picture and people

kept crouching in front of the camera. An angry Italian said something in disgust and shoved me aside. The sentiment of "Peace on earth, good will toward men" seemed far removed from this shrine of His birth.

On another day, I sat with family and friends among the rocks and grasses on a hill that overlooks Bethlehem. We read together in the scriptures, now much more alive with the places and lands they described spread out before us. First, we read of Ruth gleaning in the fields of Boaz. The hills of Moab were visible in the far distance. "Whither thou goest, I will go; and where thou lodgest, I will lodge: thy people shall be my people and thy God my God" (Ruth 1:16). We then read of Jesse and the young shepherd David being among these rocks and hills. Finally, we read of shepherds two thousand years ago watching their flocks by night, and multitudes of heavenly angels singing "Glory to God in the highest" and announcing the birth of the King of Kings, Lord of Lords, the Savior of the World. With remembered Christmas music ringing in my ears, and the scenes of Bethlehem spread out before me, I was at peace.

A fourteen-point star located in the marble floor grotto beneath the Church of the Nativity marks the alleged site where Jesus was born.

(opposite page) Evening descends on the rocks and hills of Bethlehem and Ephratah, where an angel announced the birth of Jesus to shepherds two thousand years ago.

The Church of the Nativity was first built in 385 A.D. by Helena, the mother of the Byzantine emperor Constantine. The current fortress-like structure was built in the sixth century by Justinian.

To walk today where Jesus walked is to stroll back through centuries of poignant memories to the fearful yesteryears, when Herod ruled over Judaea. (See Luke 1:5.) Although he was merely a Roman puppet, his rule was law in the land that stretched from the slopes of Mount Hermon in the north to the salt pillars bordering the Dead Sea on the south.[1] His Jewish subjects spoke longingly of a prophesied Messiah who could rescue them from Herod and foreign oppression.[2]

It was in those days—days when Herod outwardly professed to be a worshiper of Jehovah but was inwardly a man of despicable moral character—that the Gospel writer Luke began his account of wondrous, even miraculous events in Jerusalem. The initial contrast between the loving miracles of Christ's advent and the evil despotism of Herod is compelling, as are the succeeding events that fulfilled prophecy.

With the mere stroke of a pen, the physician Luke turned the attention of the world from the mighty Caesars and Herods to an elderly priest of Judaism named Zacharias, who resided with his wife Elisabeth in the hill country of Judaea near Jerusalem. Zacharias made his way to the Holy City twice each year to officiate in the temple for six days and two Sabbaths during the Jewish months that correspond to our April and October.

Among the many duties assigned to priests like Zacharias was the sacred rite of burning incense on the holy altar in the temple. Only one priest was selected to burn incense from among those who assembled in the Hall of Polished Stones to offer prescribed prayers to Jehovah. After prayers, the assembled priests followed the ancient custom of casting lots to determine which priest would be favored and chosen by God to burn incense.

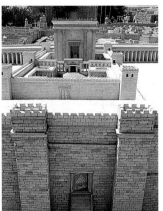

The Temple Mount as it appeared two thousand years ago is seen today in miniature at the Model City.

Interior of the Church of St. Catherine located next to the Church of the Nativity in Bethlehem.

According to the Gospel account, Zacharias received the lot. (See Luke 1:9.) While performing his duties, he saw a heavenly messenger sent from the presence of God "standing on the right side of the altar of incense" (Luke 1:11).

"Fear not, Zacharias," said the angel Gabriel to the trembling priest (Luke 1:13). "Thy prayer is heard; and thy wife Elisabeth shall bear thee a son, and thou shalt call his name John. And thou shalt have joy and gladness; and many shall rejoice at his birth. For he shall be great in the sight of the Lord . . . and he shall be filled with the Holy Ghost, even from his mother's womb" (Luke 1:13-15).3 The angel declared that the prophesied child would go before the Messiah to prepare a people for the coming of the Lord. (See Luke 1:17.)

"Whereby shall I know this?" asked Zacharias. "I am an old man, and my wife well stricken in years" (Luke 1:18). The answer given would change the course of humanity forever. A forerunner was to be conceived. A child with a promise was soon to be born to an elderly, faithful couple. An Elias was to be reared to prepare a suffering people for the Savior of the World.

Abruptly, Luke leaves the story of Zacharias, Elisabeth, and the unborn child to write of the coming forth of the Son of God. If the reader's spirit is not awakened by the angel's appearance to Zacharias, the miraculous circumstances surrounding Mary, Joseph, and the Son of God will quicken a joy, a hope, a sense of happiness not heretofore

3

A procession of pilgrims pass a cave in the Church of the Annunciation, where it is traditionally believed that the angel Gabriel appeared to Mary. (Lower photo shows exterior of the Church of the Annunciation.)

(opposite page) Still within view of the Dead Sea, Shulamit Falls, En Gedi offers refreshing relief from the desert heat. It was among these rocks and springs that David sought refuge from the threats of King Saul.

found in the written word. Luke tells of the angel Gabriel announcing to the virgin Mary that she has been chosen to be the mother of the prophesied Messiah. Luke's recounting of these events begins the greatest story in holy writ.

We assume that the virgin Mary, like other young Jewish women espoused in the "city of Galilee, named Nazareth" (Luke 1:20), had already participated in a formal betrothal ceremony. Following Jewish protocol, in the house of the betrothed-to-be a tent or booth was raised before the formal ceremony began. Inside this makeshift structure, the making sacred or the promising of the woman to the man occurred. Witnesses watched as the man gave the woman a piece of money or its equivalent and said, "Lo, thou art betrothed unto me."[4] A written document that bore his words and the woman's name was legal proof of the ceremony. When these formalities ended, the virgin Mary would be known as the wife and Joseph the carpenter as the husband through a year-long espousal period.[5]

It was during this year that the angel Gabriel came to Mary and said, "Hail, thou that art highly favoured, the Lord is with thee: blessed art thou among women. . . . And, behold, thou shalt conceive in thy womb, and bring forth a son, and shalt call his name JESUS" (Luke 1:28, 31).[6] The virgin, endowed with grace from God, answered, "Behold the handmaid of the Lord; be it unto me according to thy word" (Luke 1:38). Mary's reaction reveals her humility and her willingness to be the handmaiden of the Lord, chosen as the prophesied virgin to bear the Son of God. The child to be conceived in her womb was begotten of God, the Eternal Father, "not in violation of natural law but in accordance with a higher manifestation."[7]

We hesitate to intrude upon the sacred circumstances surrounding the conception. Let us move with Mary as she goes in haste to the hill country "into a city of Juda" (Luke 1:39), where she "entered into the house of Zacharias, and saluted Elisabeth" (Luke 1:40). That which was conceived in her womb was not hidden from her kinswoman. "Blessed art thou among women, and blessed is the fruit of thy womb," Elisabeth said as the babe within her own womb leaped for joy (Luke 1:42). She asked, "Whence is this to me, that the mother of my Lord should come to me?" (Luke 1:43).

Mary explained, "My soul doth magnify the Lord, And my spirit hath rejoiced in God my Saviour . . . from henceforth all generations shall call me blessed" (Luke 1:46-48). Mary's words revealed her knowledge of God's written word and her joy at bearing the promised Messiah.

After a prolonged absence of three months from Nazareth, Mary returned to her village on the foothills of the ancient lands of Zebulon. Her return to Nazareth was unsettling to Joseph. Mary was with child, and it appeared that she had breached the Jewish formalities of their betrothal. An annulment or divorce of the betrothal was called for in one of two ways: 1) a public trial, in which testimonies were openly expressed and a judgment rendered, or 2) a private agreement, attested by a written document known as a bill of divorce or certificate of dismissal signed in the presence of two witnesses.

"Joseph her husband, being a just man, and not willing to make her a publick example, was minded to put her away privily" (Matthew 1:19). However, such was not to be. "While he thought on these things, behold, the angel of the Lord appeared unto him in a dream, saying, Joseph, thou son of David, fear not to take unto thee Mary thy wife: for that which is conceived in her is of the Holy Ghost. And she shall bring forth a son, and thou shalt call his name JESUS: for he shall save his people from their sins" (Matthew 1:20-21).

The emotions of Joseph are not recorded by the Gospel writer Matthew, so we are left to suppose that his grave misgivings gave way to unspeakable joy as he learned that his beloved virgin was soon to be the mother of the Son of God. Matthew tells us that "Joseph being raised from sleep did as the angel of the Lord had bidden him, and took unto him his wife" (Matthew 1:24).

Scholars conclude that Mary was formally wed to Joseph before she accompanied him to Bethlehem. They base their conclusions on a Jewish custom that would not allow an espoused wife to journey unaccompanied with her husband. If their logic is correct, the Jewish wedding festivities for Joseph and Mary would have begun on the third day of the week and continued for seven days. This custom was "based on Genesis 1:9-13, where the word 'good' is used twice for the third day of creation."[8] To be married on the third day, according to the custom, was to guarantee receipt of a double blessing from God on the marriage.

Although the Gospel writer Luke failed to make mention of any marriage festivities, he was not silent about the "decree from Caesar Augustus, that all the world should be

taxed" (Luke 2:1). The Roman world subjected to the tax stretched from England on the west to the Mediterranean coastline on the east and to Africa on the south. After generations of violently enforced subjugation, Jewish men reluctantly complied with the requirement by journeying to ancient family lands to register, an important first phase of Caesar's taxation process.[9]

Among the many journeying to ancestral lands was Joseph the carpenter. Gospel writers inform us that with him on the journey was "Mary his espoused wife, being great with child" (Luke 2:5). They traveled ninety miles or a five-day journey from Nazareth to reach the outskirts of Bethlehem, the historic land of David. There they sought lodging in an inn or caravansary (khan) built to accommodate travelers who traversed the route between Jerusalem and Egypt.[10] This particular type of inn was a large, walled enclosure made of stone or sun-dried brick. According to tradition, rooms, storage chambers, and stalls in the inn surrounded a central courtyard. Inside the courtyard was a well used by travelers to fill their water bags and water their animals.

It was a well-known fact that if travelers reached the inn early in the day, they were welcomed by the innkeeper. If they arrived in the evening, the door was closed for protection and travelers were encouraged to move along. We assume that Joseph and Mary arrived at the inn during the evening, for "there was no room for them" (Luke 2:7).

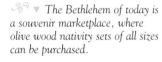

The Bethlehem of today is a souvenir marketplace, where olive wood nativity sets of all sizes can be purchased.

Shepherds still watch over their sheep today on terraced hills near Bethlehem.

(opposite page) Salt-encrusted rocks line the shores of the Dead Sea as haze hangs in the heavy air 1300 feet below sea level.

Turned away by the innkeeper, they sought lodging in one of many nearby limestone caves.[11] "And so it was, that, while they were there, the days were accomplished that she should be delivered. And she brought forth her firstborn son" (Luke 2:6-7). This newborn was the Son of God, the Messiah, the Savior of the World.

The Son of God had become as a man, subject to his parents and the traditions of society. Tradition dictated that he be wrapped in swaddling clothes. (See Luke 2:7.) Jewish mothers placed their babies on a square cloth and then began the swaddling or banding process. Four-inch-wide strips, five to six yards long, were wrapped around the infants. The swaddling restrained movement of arms and legs, which Jewish mothers believed was advantageous. They contended that the infant's appendages would "grow straight and strong" if kept in swaddling clothes.[12]

Luke tells us that Mary, as had Jewish women for centuries, wrapped her baby in swaddling clothes. But then, unlike most women, she "laid him in a manger" (Luke 2:7). The swaddling clothes and manger would be a sign to the shepherds, who, like the patriarchs of Israel—Abraham, Isaac, and Jacob—generations before abode with their flocks, "keeping watch over" them by night (Luke 2:8). To these noble men, the "glory of the Lord," even the reappearance of the ancient glory, the Shekinah, that was once seen in the Holy of Holies, "shone round about them: and they were sore afraid" (Luke 2:9).

"Fear not: for, behold, I bring you good tidings of great joy, which shall be to all people," said a holy angel. "For unto you is born this day in the city of David a Saviour, which is Christ the Lord" (Luke 2:10-11). The announced child was not just another baby born to a wandering people or to a man and woman who had come to Bethlehem to be taxed. This babe was the Son of God—the prophesied Messiah, the Holy One, the Great I AM.

As the shepherds listened to the angelic message, "suddenly there was with the angel a multitude of the heavenly host praising God, and saying, Glory to God in the highest, and on earth peace, good will toward men" (Luke 2:13-14). When the angel departed, the shepherds went in haste to the limestone cave near Bethlehem, and there they "found Mary, and Joseph, and the babe lying in a manger" (Luke 2:16). After seeing "what the Lord hath made known" to them, they glorified and praised God and told others about the holy birth (Luke 2:15).

Luke tells us that in conformity to the Hebrew law, Jesus was brought by Mary and Joseph to be circumcised eight days after his birth as a sign of the Abrahamic covenant. (See Exodus 12:48-49; Luke 2:21.) Thirty-two days later, "when the days of her purification according to the law of Moses were accomplished," they brought Jesus to Jerusalem to present him before a priest serving at the Gate of Nicanor on the Temple Mount—the Har Habayit, the House of God (Luke 2:22).[13] This presentation to a priest, like circumcision, was expected of Jewish parents, as was Mary's purification offering of "a pair of turtledoves, or two young pigeons" (Luke 2:24).

After or as the offering was given, Simeon, a devout and just man, who knew "by the Holy Ghost, that he should not see death, before he had seen the Lord's Christ" recognized Jesus as the long-awaited Messiah (Luke 2:26). He lovingly took the newborn in his arms and praised God, saying, "Lord, now lettest thou thy servant depart in peace . . . For mine eyes have seen thy salvation" (Luke 2:29-30). Simeon knew that Jesus was "a light to lighten the Gentiles and the glory of thy people Israel" (Luke 2:32). He understood the atoning mission of the babe— the "child is set for the fall and rising again of many in Israel" (Luke 2:34).

In a moment, Anna, an elderly prophetess, who had "served God with fastings and prayers night and day . . . gave thanks likewise unto the Lord" for the child (Luke 2:37-38). These two faithful servants of God, like shepherds before them, were witnesses of Jesus; and like the shepherds, Anna spoke about the child "to all them that looked for redemption in Jerusalem" (Luke 2:38).

Simeon and Anna were not the last witnesses of the advent of the Christ child. Wise men from the east were coming to Jerusalem. Legend sets their number anywhere from three to twelve. They were following a star or the direction of the star, possibly in fulfillment of the ancient prophecy that "there shall come a Star out of Jacob, and a

▲ Mt. Hermon, the highest mount in Israel, rises from the lush, green highlands of the Golan Heights along the northern border.

◄ (opposite page) Nazareth is located on steep hillsides about halfway between the Sea of Galilee and the Mediterranean seaport of Haifa.

Sceptre shall rise out of Israel" (Numbers 24:17). Arriving in Jerusalem, they sought audience with King Herod. "Where is he that is born King of the Jews? for we have seen his star in the east, and are come to worship him," they asked (Matthew 2:2). Their words implied that Herod, the Roman appointee and exploiter of Judaism, was aware of a prophesied star that would appear at the birth of a king.

Herod, unaware of the star, "gathered all the chief priests and scribes of the people together, [and] demanded of them where Christ should be born" (Matthew 2:4). The answer he received from scholars of the Torah was "Bethlehem, in the land of Juda" (Matthew 2:6. See Micah 5:2). With veiled deception, he encouraged the wise men to "Go and search diligently for the young child [in Bethlehem]; and when ye have found him, bring me word again, that I may come and worship him also" (Matthew 2:8).

The wise men left the Roman appointee, and once again "the star, which they saw in the east, went before them, till it came and stood over where the young child was" (Matthew 2:9). Entering the house, they saw the child Jesus and "fell down, and worshipped him" (Matthew 2:11). Then and only then did they open their precious gifts that had been carefully carried from the east. According to medieval tradition, each gift had a symbolic meaning. Gold acknowledged that Jesus was king. Incense or frankincense symbolized his priestly role, and myrrh represented his atoning death. If the tradition has validity, in the gifts of the wise men the divine mission of Jesus the Christ—the Anointed One—was symbolized.

The wise men did not return to Herod with news of finding the child born to be king. They were "warned of God in a dream that they should not return" (Matthew 2:12). In obedience the wise men journeyed back to their eastern lands, and were never mentioned again in scripture.

▲ *The courtyard of St. Catherine's Church includes a statue commemorating St. Jerome's writing of the Vulgate.*

◄ *The Church of Dormition ("Falling Asleep of the Virgin") is believed to be where Mary died. It is located on Mount Zion, where many sacred sites of both Christianity and Judaism are found.*

◄ *(opposite page) Within view of Bethlehem (Bet Lehem, literally meaning "house of bread") are fields of grain, not unlike those where Ruth and Naomi gleaned in the fields of Boaz.*

11

CHAPTER 2

Out of Egypt

▶ *The ancient Nile flows in quiet contrast through the modern city of Cairo, Egypt.*

▶ *(opposite page) It is estimated that the pyramids of Giza were built over two thousand years before the child Jesus was brought to Egypt.*

PHOTOGRAPHER'S NOTE - APRIL 16, 1998
ARRIVAL IN EGYPT AND THE NILE

Sixteen hours of sitting in an airplane, added to six more hours in the Salt Lake, New York, and Vienna airports, have not prepared me for the scene taking place outside my window. It's midnight, and I am twelve stories above a noisy "round about" circular intersection on the west side of the Nile in Cairo, Egypt. One would think that sleep would be a welcome relief after going without it for nearly twenty-four hours, but thoughts are racing through my mind, like the noisy, honking cars coming and going in an endless stream of humanity along both sides of the Nile.

In the hustle and bustle of this modern metropolis, the Nile still flows in quiet contrast. Only the reflected lights of a thousand street lamps float on her surface this night. The silt-laden water has given life to this desert country for over five thousand years. The Nile that carried Moses in a basket of reeds, and greeted Joseph who was sold into Egypt, may have also bathed the child Jesus.

I return to bed, but sleep is as far away as the familiar surroundings of home. Back on the balcony, I set up the camera and photograph the night and the city. From the nearby minaret of a Moslem mosque, an Islamic invitation to prayer is sung over loudspeakers, amplified and distorted to an almost deafening volume. A haze of pollution builds over the ancient city as the first light in the eastern sky begins to glow.

I finally succumb to sleep, but only for a few hours. The full light of morning finds me back on the balcony, scanning the scene below. The buildings look stained by the dusty air. Only a few cars go by in the early morning. But now and again, a horse-drawn cart driven by an Egyptian farmer dressed in a full-length, shirt-like garment and turban scarf slowly makes its way across a bridge over the Nile. A beggar woman with a child in her lap seeks a handout. A man fishes from the bridge over the Nile. Cars go by, honking at the strangeness of an American with a camera in this early morning hour. Visual elements of contrasting time periods merge to form the fabric of this Egyptian picture that I find myself walking through.

The ancient Nile River flowing through Luxor has given life to Egypt for more than five thousand years.

Not far from the fertile valleys and hillsides of Jerusalem is the vast wilderness of the Judaean desert. John the Baptist preached repentance in the wilderness, and Jesus was led by the Spirit into the wilderness to fast for forty days and nights in preparation for his ministry. The temperature when taking this photograph was about 115 degrees.

After the wise men departed into their own country, an "angel of the Lord appeareth to Joseph in a dream" and said, "Arise, and take the young child and his mother, and flee into Egypt, and be thou there until I bring thee word: for Herod will seek the young child to destroy him" (Matthew 2:13). Obedient to the angelic command, and with the cover of night to cloak their escape, Joseph took Mary and the child Jesus away from Bethlehem, crossing the Sinai and Negev deserts to reach Egypt. In the land that boasted of pyramids and past greatness, Joseph, Mary, and the child Jesus found a home.

Joseph's obedience to the angelic words spoken in Bethlehem saved the life of Jesus. When the wise men failed to return with information of the newborn king, Herod "saw that he was mocked of the wise men, [and] was exceeding wroth" (Matthew 2:16). In anger, he ordered the slaying of "all the children that were in Bethlehem, and in all the coasts thereof, from two years old and under" (Matthew 2:16). The foreordained John, son of Zacharias and Elisabeth, escaped the intended soldier's blade when Elisabeth took him from Bethlehem into the mountainous wilderness. Zacharias was not so fortunate, however; he was slain by Herod's soldiers between the porch and altar of the temple for refusing to reveal the hiding place of his wife and son. This tragedy, together with the killing of the innocent infants, was but one of many cruel atrocities credited to Herod.[1] No wonder there were expressions of joy at Herod's death.

Joseph learned of Herod's death from a heavenly messenger who appeared to him in a dream. "Arise, and take the young child and his mother, and go into the land of Israel: for they are dead which sought the young child's life," said the angel (Matthew 2:20). Again, Joseph listened and obeyed. He left Egypt and returned with Mary and Jesus across the deserts to Palestine.

When they entered the borders of Palestine, they learned that Herod's domain had been divided between his three errant sons—Archelaus, Philipp, and Antipas. Archelaus was now the Roman appointed king over Judaea, Samaria, and Jerusalem. Philipp was reigning as tetrarch over the territory northeast of the Sea of Galilee. And Antipas ruled as tetrarch of Galilee and Peraea. "When [Joseph] heard that Archelaus did reign in Judaea in the room of his father Herod, he was afraid to go thither [and] . . . turned aside into the parts of Galilee" where Herod Antipas ruled (Matthew 2:22). There, Joseph and Mary made a home for Jesus in "their own city Nazareth" (Luke 2:39).

In this agrarian community, the child "grew, and waxed strong in spirit, filled with wisdom: and the grace of God was upon him" (Luke 2:40). Although the childhood and youth of Jesus are virtually obscured in silence, there are a few assumptions that can be made. First, Jesus was raised in a Jewish household. Most Jewish homes at that time had a folded piece of parchment located on the doorpost. The words on the parchment read, "Hear, O Israel: The Lord our God is one Lord: And thou shalt love the Lord thy God with all thine heart, and with all thy soul, and with all thy might" (Deuteronomy 6:4-5). These verses were a reminder to those who entered the home to hear and listen to the word of God. As members of the household entered or left the home, they touched the parchment with a finger, then touched their lips with the same finger as a symbolic remembrance and prayer to God.

Other Jewish symbols of home worship at that time were lullabies based on the Book of Psalm and selected teachings from the writings of ancient prophets. Mothers sang lullabies while fathers taught scriptural passages, prayers, and wise

sayings to their sons. We assume that the parchment, lullabies, and scriptural teachings were an important part of the childhood of Jesus.

After reaching the age of six or seven, young Jewish boys in Nazareth received an education at the local synagogue. Although the education included reading, writing, and arithmetic, the principal topic of study was the legal observance of Judaism. To the rabbi who taught in the synagogue, "the knowledge of God was everything; and to prepare for or impart that knowledge was the sum total, the sole object of his education."[2]

Another Jewish symbol of worship was attendance at festivals in Jerusalem. The law required all Jewish males to present themselves at the Passover festivities, whereas Jewish women were asked only to attend Passover "if not lawfully detained."[3] For a Jewish man or woman to journey to Jerusalem for Passover was always to make a pilgrimage, meaning to travel in a caravan with others of their faith. The caravan was an elaborate affair in which an elected leader began the pilgrimage by shouting, "Arise ye, and let us go up to Zion, to the House of our God."[4] Joyful followers arose and sang hymns of praise from the Book of Psalm as they went up to Jerusalem. The rich in the caravan drove chariots, the afflicted rode beasts of burden, but most journeyed on foot, believing it "more meritorious to make the pilgrimage that way."[5] At the time of Jesus, great multitudes of Jews—nearly 100,000—made a sacred pilgrimage to Jerusalem for the Passover festivities.

When Jesus was twelve years old, he was one of the multitude that went up to Jerusalem "after the custom of the feast" (Luke 2:42). Luke's mention of "the custom of the feast" refers to the Jewish law that required every twelve-year-old male to be formally presented to a priest serving on the Temple Mount (Luke 2:42). The priest had the respon-

▲ *Young Jewish boys are brought to the temple for Bar Mitzvah ceremonies when they are about twelve or thirteen years old.*

▲ *Interior of a historic synagogue in the Old City of Jerusalem.*

15

▲ Christian pilgrims come to Yardenit to be baptized, believing that this site was where Jesus was baptized.

▲ Anciently, the temple was built on top of the wall as shown in the miniature at the Model City.

▶ Immersion as a purification rite was practiced by the Jews before the time of John the Baptist and Jesus of Nazareth. This is an immersion pool at Masada.

sibility of pronouncing young males "Sons of the Law." This important title gave young men the right to hold a position in a local synagogue, be recognized as a member of the community, choose a vocation, enter into advanced studies, and no longer be sold as bond servants by their parents. These were the temporal blessings. The eternal blessing was the most sought after by the young men. It was a promise that the young would one day dine with the patriarchs of Israel—Abraham, Isaac, and Jacob—at a future Messianic feast.

When all the customs of Passover ended, pilgrims returned to their homes rejoicing at having been in Jerusalem. Among the pilgrims returning to Nazareth that year were Joseph and Mary. They were unaware that "the child Jesus tarried behind in Jerusalem" (Luke 2:43). Believing that Jesus was in their company, they went a day's journey before discovering he was not with the other pilgrims. (See Luke 2:44.)[6] "And when they found him not, they turned back again to Jerusalem, seeking him" (Luke 2:45).

Three days passed before Jesus was found. Mary discovered him on the Temple Mount, "sitting in the midst of the doctors, both hearing them, and asking them questions. And all that heard him were astonished at his understanding and answers" (Luke 2:46-47). This scene of a young Jewish male talking with learned doctors was not atypical on the Temple Mount. Ancient Jewish records reveal occasional instances of precocious young men conversing with and learning from rabbis, scribes, and doctors who had written interpretive commentary and narratives of the law—halakah, the legal commentary, and haggadah, the traditional commentary. What is unusual is the *Joseph Smith Translation* of the incident, which reports that "they [the doctors] were hearing him, and asking him questions" (JST, Luke 2:46).

This interpretation helps explain why "when [Joseph and Mary] saw him, they were amazed" (Luke 2:48). Mary asked her son, "Why hast thou thus dealt with us? behold, thy father and I have sought thee sorrowing" (Luke 2:48). Jesus answered, "How is it that ye sought me? wist ye not that I must be about my Father's business?" (Luke 2:49). These questions, the first recorded words of Jesus, reveal his knowledge of his true parentage. Yet Joseph and Mary "understood not the saying which he spake unto them" (Luke 2:50).

Jesus left the Temple Mount and the Holy City with Joseph and Mary. The time had not come for his ministry to begin. It remained for him to complete a season of preparation within a family of brothers and sisters. (See Matthew 13:55.) We assume that the preparation included tutoring

by Joseph. Tradition suggests that he taught Jesus a trade, as was customary for Jewish fathers. (See Mark 6:3.) It was also during these years that "Jesus increased in wisdom and stature, and in favour with God and man" (Luke 2:52).

As he increased in the important attainments of life, our attention turns from Jesus to his kinsman John, who was "preaching in the wilderness of Judaea, . . . Prepare ye the way of the Lord, make his paths straight" (Matthew 3:1, 3). His simple message—repent and be baptized— could not be misconstrued. (See Luke 3:3.) When he cried repentance, he was asking the people to return to the covenants between God and their ancient fathers—Abraham, Isaac, and Jacob. Those who repented were welcomed into the

The Jordan River is formed from run-off water from Mount Hermon and from springs and babbling brooks in the nature preserve located on the ancient land of the tribe of Dan. In Hebrew, the word for going down is "Yored." The water of this river is referred to as "Yored-Dan," or Jordan.

waters of baptism, and John became known throughout Judaea as the Baptist. His message was so simple, yet powerful, that many sought baptism from him and turned away from the teachings of Pharisees and Sadducees.

The prideful Pharisees and Sadducees were angry at the loss of followers and sought occasion to see John. To these men, who wore soft garments, flowing robes, and linen girdles, John said, "O generation of vipers, who hath warned you to flee from the wrath to come?" (Matthew 3:7). His portrayal of Pharisees and Sadducees as poisonous snakes that destroyed the spiritual longings of the Jewish people fueled their anger, as did his simple attire of a "raiment of camel's hair, and a leathern girdle about his loins" (Matthew 3:4). Yet they were powerless to regain the hearts of the people, who were being prepared for the ministry of the Lord Jesus.

To the repentant who listened to John, it seemed "that all men mused in their hearts of John, whether he were the Christ, or not" (Luke 3:15). In answer to their musings, John confessed, "I indeed baptize you with water; but one mightier than I cometh, the latchet of whose shoes I am not worthy to unloose: he shall baptize you with the Holy Ghost and with fire" (Luke 3:16). By this statement John equated himself with the lowest household servant, whose task it was to unloose sandals or latchets on his master's shoes. John knew that although he was the promised son of Zacharias and Elisabeth, he was merely a servant compared to the Son of God.

As John spoke to the multitudes of his humility and the greatness of the Messiah, "then cometh Jesus from Galilee to Jordan unto John, to be baptized of him" (Matthew 3:13). John's initial reaction to the request for baptism was to refuse. "I have need to be baptized of thee," he said (Matthew 3:14). Jesus answered, "Suffer it to be so

▼ *This pile of stones is located in a remote area of the Judaean desert near Wadi Qelt. "If thou be the Son of God, command that these stones be made bread," was the first satanic temptation (Matthew 4:3).*

▲ *At the pinnacle of the temple, Satan again tried to tempt Jesus. The Greek word for pinnacle is patrux, meaning "wing" or "extension." Many scholars contend that Jesus was on the roof of the temple rather than standing on the wall.*

▶ *The Western Wall (Wailing Wall) is the most significant artifact in Jerusalem for religious Jews today. The wall is a reminder of the ancient temple enclosure that dominated the Temple Mount during the days of Solomon and the reign of Herod the Great.*

now: for thus it becometh us to fulfill all righteousness" (Matthew 3:15). Symbolically, the baptism of Jesus by his kinsman John represents the depth of his humility and his willingness to fulfill the law of God. After his baptism, "[Jesus] went up straightway out of the water: and, lo, the heavens were opened unto him, and he saw the Spirit of God descending like a dove, and lighting upon him" (Matthew 3:16).

The dove, given as a sign for the two most important baptisms in the world—the baptism of Jesus and the baptism of the earth—witnessed to John the presence of the Spirit of God. The dove was a sign to him that Jesus was the Son of God, just as the dove was a manifestation to Noah that God had "made peace with the earth."[7] (See Matthew 3:16; Genesis 8:8-12.) After the baptism, a voice was heard from heaven: "This is my beloved Son, in whom I am well pleased" (Matthew 3:17). The joy of that day—that holy day in which Jesus, the Perfect One, accepted the baptism of repentance and the voice of God was heard from heaven—was unparalleled.

Jesus, "being full of the Holy Ghost" from the events of that glorious day, left Jordan and was "led by the Spirit into the wilderness" (Luke 4:1). His purpose was to fast, to pray, and to commune with God.

For the next forty days and forty nights, Jesus "did eat nothing: and when they were ended, he afterward hungered" (Luke 4:2). In his weakened physical state, the devil assaulted him in that mountainous wilderness with temptations designed to undermine his submission to the will of God.[8] "If thou be the Son of God, command that these stones be made bread," the arch-deceiver demanded (Matthew 4:3). The satanic temptation for Jesus to succumb to his carnal appetite was contrary to the childhood lessons of Judaism, in which every aspect of life—even the

necessary act of eating—was in subjection to the spiritual realm. Jesus acknowledged the temptation by paraphrasing the words of Moses, "Man doth not live by bread only," and then declared to Satan the source of life—"every word that proceedeth out of the mouth of the Lord" (Deuteronomy 8:3). Then Jesus was taken by the Spirit to an "exceeding high mountain," and after he had seen the "kingdoms of the world, and the glory of them," again the devil appeared (Matthew 4:8). "All these things will I give thee, if thou wilt fall down and worship me," he said (Matthew 4:9). Jesus answered, "Get thee behind me, Satan: for it is written, Thou shalt worship the Lord thy God, and him only shalt thou serve" (Luke 4:8).

The Spirit next took Jesus to the pinnacle of the temple, and there the adversary came again, saying, "If thou be the Son of God, cast thyself down from hence: For it is written, He shall give his angels charge over thee, to keep thee" (Luke 4:9-10). The Savior's answer, "Thou shalt not tempt the Lord thy God," caused the devil to depart from him (Luke 4:12). His triumphant victory over the satanic temptations in the wilderness was complete.

He then left the wilderness and journeyed to Galilee "in the power of the Spirit" (Luke 4:14). The fame and reputation of Jesus spread throughout the region, and his ministry—the ministry of the Son of God—commenced.

The lights of the Old City glow at dawn above Jerusalem. Taken near the Orson Hyde Park on the Mount of Olives.

CHAPTER 3

THE SHORES OF GALILEE

PHOTOGRAPHER'S NOTE - MAY 7, 1998
KIBBUTZ NEAR NAZARETH

The heat has been oppressive. Coupled with the wind, it is like the forced air of a furnace blowing on sunburned skin. Seeking shade, I find only shade—not escape from the heat. I am told it is unusually hot for this time of year. Hot winds blow through the trees, flowers, and fields, blowing with it dust that fills the air and filters my view of the Sea of Galilee. Squinting to protect my eyes from flying bits of grit doesn't improve the scene.

Driving into Nazareth, I escape neither the heat nor wind. Nazareth is set on steep hillsides, more mountainous than hills. It is in Arab-controlled Israel today. Multi-level block houses and apartments cover the steep slopes, creating a cramped feeling as I drive up and down narrow roads that wind through crevasses and canyons. Nazareth has all the charm of a mining town in Nevada or Colorado. It feels dirty on this dry, hot, windy day.

I strain to find signs of a carpenter shop, but see only garages, gas stations, and food markets. Churches mark the spot

where the angel appeared to Mary, and where the boy Jesus went to synagogue. Another marks his childhood home. I saw the quarry where the multitude threatened to stone Jesus when he told them who he was.

Driving out of town, I find myself wondering, "Can there any good thing come out of Nazareth?" (John 1:46). Maybe the cooler conditions of another day will cast a different light on the name of Nazareth.

"Repent: for the kingdom of heaven is at hand," said Jesus in villages and cities bordering the Sea of Galilee (Matthew 4:17).[1] His message was not new; repentance had been the focus of John the Baptist's ministry. But his invitation, "Follow me, and I will make you fishers of men," was new and intriguing to those who heard it (Matthew 4:19).

Without hesitation, "straightway [Andrew and Simon] left their nets, and followed him" (Matthew 4:20). James and John "immediately left [their] ship and their father, and followed him" (Matthew 4:22). Jesus' invitation to Philip

Homes and apartments built on the hillsides of Nazareth with a fig tree in the foreground.

(opposite page) Sunset on the Sea of Galilee at En Gev, looking toward Tiberias.

of Bethsaida added yet another disciple. Philip, in turn, spoke to Nathanael, declaring that "We have found him, of whom Moses in the law, and the prophets, did write, Jesus of Nazareth, the son of Joseph."[2] Each disciple knew with Andrew, "We have found the Messias" (John 1:41). Thus, one by one, followers of Jesus were gathered along the shores of Galilee from among the tradesmen, the commoners.

These men willingly left their vocations and cares of the world to follow Jesus of Nazareth. Some even went with him to a wedding feast held in Kfar Cana of Galilee. (See John 2:1-2.) Although tradition suggests that Jesus and his disciples attended the wedding feast of a local farmer, not all agree. Conjecture over who was married in Cana that day does not negate the presence of Jesus at the feast or that he "set the seal of His approval upon the matrimonial relationship and upon the propriety of social entertainment."[3]

Perhaps it was the length of the wedding festivities in Cana (such a celebration often lasted more than a day) that

▼ Large clay (terra-cotta) water jar, not unlike what was used at the wedding feast in Cana.

explains why Mary, "the mother of Jesus saith unto [her son], They have no wine" (John 2:3). But it is important to note that Jewish custom demanded wine be offered to wedding guests. To have marriage festivities without the needed wine was to bring misfortune to the marriage. It seems apparent that although water was a precious commodity to desert travelers, Mary recognized that wine from the fruit of the vine was needed to satisfy the guests.

Jesus said to his mother, "Woman, what have I to do with thee? mine hour is not yet come" (John 2:4).[4] Yet, he who had triumphed over Satan's temptation to abate his own hunger in the wilderness responded affirmatively to his mother's plea. He said to the household servants, "Fill the waterpots with water" (John 2:7). The servants filled the six stone pots to their brims. Jesus then told the servants, "Draw out now, and bear unto the governor of the feast" (John 2:8).[5] After drinking the wine brought by the servants, the governor said to the groom, "Thou hast kept the good wine until now" (John 2:10). He did not know that the wine he drank had been miraculously provided by Jesus of Nazareth. He did not know that this miracle was the first of thirty-six recorded miracles attributed to Jesus by Gospel writers. But the disciples of Jesus knew that he had provided this luxury for the wedding guests, whose thirst was only momentary. He had "manifested forth his glory; and his disciples believed on him" (John 2:11).

They left the festivities and journeyed down to Capernaum, a lakeside community on the major trade route between Damascus and Alexandria. Their stay was brief, as it was nearing Passover again, and like other Jewish males, Jesus and his disciples were expected in Jerusalem. Rather than delay, they left Capernaum soon after their arrival and made a pilgrimage to the Holy City.

There were more miracles attributed to Jesus in Capernaum than any other village or city in Galilee.

Architectural fragments found in Capernaum showing the Megan David—Star of David.

Money changers are still seen today near the Temple Mount.

Capernaum was located on the northern shore of the Sea of Galilee.

(opposite page) The walls of the Old City of Jerusalem have been built layer upon layer over several millennia.

In Jerusalem, instead of blending in with thousands of pilgrims crowding the marketplaces and even the Temple Mount, Jesus dramatically made his presence known. The setting was the Mount, on which a complex of courtyards was used by Jewish merchants as a thriving marketplace. Market stalls within the courtyards contained sacrificial doves, pigeons, and lambs for sale to the highest bidder. The ceremonial fitness of the birds and animals was loudly extolled by merchants, who expected and charged exorbitant prices. Near the boisterous merchants sat money changers. These men were eager to make a profit trading foreign coins, the legal tender used by Jews for temporal purposes, for half shekels—the only monetary denomination accepted by temple priests as offerings.

Reacting to the profiteering on the Temple Mount, Jesus improvised a whip of small cords and lashed out against merchandising and money changing so near the Holy Temple. With the whip he drove both man and animal from the Court of the Gentiles. He "poured out the changers' money, and overthrew the tables" (John 2:15). He said to those who sold doves, "Take these things hence; make not my Father's house an house of merchandise" (John 2:16).

Even though his bold actions disrupted business on the Temple Mount and led to a loss of merchandise, there is no record of his being stopped, arrested, or criticized by Roman rulers or Jewish leaders. Only a question of credentials was raised. "What sign shewest thou unto us, seeing that thou doest these things?" (John 2:18).

Why was no legal action taken against Jesus? The answer lies in the Jews' negative opinion of merchandising practices on the Mount. Jesus' actions appealed to Jewish sentiment, and many now "believed in his name" (John 2:23). Others, like the Pharisee Nicodemus, were not ready to admit that Jesus was the Son of God, but did recognize him as a great teacher.

Jesus left the Holy City after Passover, leaving behind disgruntled merchants and money changers and the contemplative Nicodemus. He journeyed to the land of Judaea and tarried there for a short season. It was while in Judaea that Jesus heard that his kinsman John had been cast into prison. According to the Jewish historian Josephus, "John was sent in chains to the fortress of Machaerus" located on the mountain slope east of the Dead Sea.[6] His imprisonment stemmed from his denunciation of the unlawful marriage of Herod Antipas to Herodias.

When Jesus heard of John's imprisonment, he left Judaea and departed into Galilee. (See Matthew 4:12; John 4:3.) As he journeyed toward Galilee, he passed through the land of Samaria—an unusual route for a Jew traveling to Galilee or any other destination. To the Jews, Samaritans were a despised people, and it seems unusual, if not inappropriate, that Jesus would take his disciples through Samaritan lands. Yet, there was a purpose. Near the city of Sychar, as Jesus sat on Jacob's well, a Samaritan woman approached the well to draw water. Jesus said to her, "Give me to drink" (John 4:7). Instead of responding to his request, the woman asked, "How is it that thou, being a Jew, askest drink of me, which am a woman of Samaria?" (John 4:9) In other words, why would a Jew with a tradition of hatred toward Samaritans make a request of a Samaritan woman? Jesus answered, "If thou knewest the gift of God, and who it is that saith to thee, Give me to drink; thou wouldest have asked of him, and he would have given thee living water" (John 4:10).

A discussion ensued between Jesus and the woman at the well until the woman concluded, "Sir, I perceive that thou art a prophet" (John 4:19). Jesus corrected her perception and announced that he was the Messiah: "I that speak unto thee am he" (John 4:26). The astonished woman left Jesus and went to the city, saying, "Come, see a man" (John 4:29). Many in the city came to Jacob's well and listened to Jesus and "believed on him . . . that this is indeed the Christ, the Saviour of the world" (John 4:39).

After two days in Samaria, Jesus continued his journey toward Galilee. When he arrived in Cana, he was approached by an official of Herod Antipas requesting his presence in Capernaum to "heal his son: for he was at the point of death" (John 4:47). "Sir, come down ere my child die," he pleaded. Jesus responded, "Go thy way; thy son liveth" (John 4:49-50). And it was so. The son was the blessed recipient of Jesus' second miracle in Cana. The nobleman and his household, like the Samaritans in

The Mount of Precipitation or Mount of Jumping is marked by a Byzantine church. This may be the quarry where angry Nazarenes tried to stone Jesus.

The Herodian walls of the Old City are built of limestone blocks.

Sychar, joined a growing throng of believers. "And there went out a fame of him through all the region round about. And he taught in their synagogues, being glorified of all" (Luke 4:14-15).

The exception to "glorified of all" happened in Nazareth, the village of his childhood and youth. It was on a Sabbath day—a holy day when devout Jews joyously remembered and observed the goodness of God. It was on the day when rabbis symbolically spoke of the Sabbath as a bride. "All the days of the week," the rabbis claimed, "has God paired, except the Sabbath, which is alone, that it may be wedded to Israel."[7]

During Sabbath in Nazareth, as in other villages throughout Judaea, fine clothes were worn, delicious meals were eaten, the Torah was studied, and lectures on religious topics were attended. It was a day for praising God. Fasting and mourning were forbidden, as were claims of fatigue and illness. This was a day of peace and joy, not a day for disharmony or petition.

On this serene day in Nazareth, Jesus "went into the synagogue" (Luke 4:16). The interior of the building was divided between the Most Holy and the Holy areas, much like the temple built by Solomon and the ancient tabernacle of Moses. Located in the Most Holy area was an ark that held the Books of Moses, a raised platform with a reading desk that faced the ark, an eight-branched lamp, and chief seats. (See Matthew 23:6.) The Holy area had a separate entrance for men and women. A partition, often a grating, ensured that men and women did not mingle during the worship service.

After a series of prescribed formalities, the rabbi lifted the scroll of the Books of Moses from the ark, and seven members of the congregation were invited to read scriptural passages from the scroll at the reading desk.

▼ *Olive press near the Synagogue at Capernaum.*

▲ *Capernaum, and neighboring Chorazim, or Bethsaida, were cursed by Jesus. Today there are only fragments of the once thriving cities.*

◄ *Garden area with statue in Capernaum.*

29

The first invited to read was a descendant of Aaron, the second a descendant of Levi, and the remaining five were descendants of the other sons of the House of Israel. Each reading was preceded and followed by a brief benediction. Then extracts from the prophetic books were read— "Joshua, Judges, Samuel, Kings, Isaiah, Jeremiah, Ezekiel, or the twelve minor prophets."[8] (See Luke 24:27.)

When "some great Rabbi, or famed preacher, or else a distinguished stranger, was known to be in the town," it was customary to invite him to be a reader.[9] As the fame of Jesus had spread through the Galilee region, he was one who "stood up for to read" (Luke 4:16). This courtesy or recognition may have been granted because popular preachers were given freedom to teach "parables, stories, allegories, witticisms, strange and foreign words, absurd legends, in short, anything that might startle an audience."[10] Or it may have been granted because of past memories of Joseph, Mary, and Jesus in their community.

As Jesus stepped forward to read, "there was delivered unto him the book" or scrolls (Luke 4:17). When Jesus read from the scroll of Isaiah, given him by the attendant of the synagogue, he paraphrased the written Hebrew. He then expanded and interpreted the scriptural passages. This was not unusual, for each reader was expected to expound upon the scripture he read.

Jesus "found the place where it was written, The Spirit of the Lord is upon me, because he hath anointed me to preach the gospel to the poor; he hath sent me to heal the broken hearted, to preach deliverance to the captives, and recovering of sight to the blind, to set at liberty them that are bruised, To preach the acceptable year of the Lord" (Luke 4:17-19). Jesus then "closed the book, and he gave it again to the [attendant], and sat down. And the eyes of all them that were in the synagogue were fastened on him" (Luke 4:20). He then said, "This day is this scripture ful-filled in your ears" (Luke 4:21).

"And all bare him witness, and wondered at the gracious words which proceedeth out of his mouth. And they said, Is not this Joseph's son?" (Luke 4:22). They mused over the absurdity of Joseph's son being the Messiah. Jesus responded to their musings by stating, "No prophet is accepted in his own country" (Luke 2:24). "When they heard these things, [they] were filled with wrath" (Luke 4:28). We assume that they did not allow Jesus to conclude his comments with the traditional benediction. Instead, they "rose up, and thrust him out of the city, and led him unto the brow of the hill whereon their city was built, that they might cast him down headlong" (Luke 4:29).

The villagers, many of whom may have known Jesus from early childhood, intended to kill him in what was known as a "Rebel's Beating." The beating was not hitting or clubbing, but crowding the victim over a cliff at least twice a man's height. By simply crowding him to fall from the cliff, no one person in the angry mob could be held accountable for the deadly consequence. If he were pushed over the cliff by a single individual, accountability for death under the Jewish law was mandatory.

Although their murderous plans were thwarted when Jesus "passing through the midst of them went his way," this Sabbath in Nazareth would mar the village forever (Luke 4:30). The same village in which the angel Gabriel had announced to Mary the coming of the Messiah had turned and rejected their Lord, and Nazareth would become a hiss and a byword for generations.

It is possible that Jesus never returned to the village of his childhood. The Gospel writers tell of his restless existence in villages and towns near the Sea of Galilee. "Foxes have holes, and birds of the air have nests; but the Son of man hath not where to lay his head" (Luke 9:58).

▲ *Light from the setting sun streams heavenward as seen from the Mount of Beatitudes.*

◀ *(opposite page) The brilliant blossoms of a bougainvillea bush beautify the shoreline of the Sea of Galilee at the Kibbutz of En Gev.*

CHAPTER 4

FROM THE SEA TO THE MOUNT

Red poppies cover the fertile hills and valleys of Israel each spring.

(opposite page) Flowers adorn the shoreline of the Mediterranean Sea at Ashkelon, where Samson killed thirty Philistines (and later a thousand Philistines with the jawbone of an ass). (Judges 14-15)

PHOTOGRAPHER'S NOTE - MAY 6, 1998
SERMON ON THE MOUNT

In my mind I can see Jesus seated on the Mount of Beatitudes, teaching his twelve apostles about his and their mission. The hillside is covered with grasses of green, with hundreds, even thousands of rich red spring flowers fluttering in the breeze as he lovingly teaches, "Consider the lilies of the field, how they grow; they toil not, neither do they spin: And yet I say unto you, That even Solomon in all his glory was not arrayed like one of these" (Matthew 6:28-29).

A few days later, in Gethsemane, I see poppies of red dotting the ground under the olive trees. They remind me of the great drops of blood that were shed for the sins of all—for me. Suddenly, the importance of the Savior's teaching is clear. Of course, Solomon in all his glory was not arrayed as one of these, for these spring flowers are brilliant reminders of the Atonement.

Although rejected in the synagogue at Nazareth, Jesus did not avoid teaching in the synagogue in Capernaum, where four future apostles—Peter, Andrew, James, and John—and their families worshiped. As they listened to the Lord, they "were astonished at his doctrine: for he taught them as one that had authority" (Mark 1:22). Among those assembled was a man who cried out, "Let us alone, what have we to do with thee, thou Jesus of Nazareth? art thou come to destroy us? I know thee who thou art, the Holy One of God" (Mark 1:24).

Jesus rebuked the declaration when he commanded, "Hold thy peace" (Luke 4:35). His rebuke was directed toward the unclean spirit within the man, for such a proclamation from one influenced by Satan was not a statement of a believing witness. Jesus ordered the evil spirit to "come out of him" (Mark 1:25). "And when the devil had thrown him in the midst, he came out of him, and hurt him not" (Luke 4:35).

A modern replica of an ancient fishing boat on the Sea of Galilee.

were healed, scant details remain of their afflictions or healings. Two notable exceptions are the man suffering with leprosy and the man afflicted with palsy.

The leper suffered from a skin disease that had deteriorated his body humors. Although devout Jews would consider the leprous man a sinner and avoid any contact with him, Jesus would not. As the leper approached the Master, he said, "Lord, if thou wilt, thou canst make me clean" (Matthew 8:2). Unafraid of his leprosy, Jesus "put forth his hand, and touched him" (Matthew 8:3). "Be thou clean," he declared, "and immediately his leprosy was cleansed" (Matthew 8:3).

The man suffering from palsy, like the leper, was believed to be afflicted with the malady because of past sins. However, this man, unlike the leper, had four friends who ignored societal stigma and carried the man on a bed—a mat, handwoven rug, or litter—searching for Jesus. They found the Lord preaching in a crowded home, where "there was no room to receive" others (Mark 2:2). The friends were not deterred by the situation.

"And when they could not come nigh unto him for the press, they uncovered the roof" or awning of the home, and "let down the bed wherein the sick of the palsy lay" (Mark 2:4). As Jesus witnessed their actions in behalf of the palsied man, he was moved with compassion. (See Mark 2:5.) "Son, be of good cheer; thy sins be forgiven thee. . . . Arise, and take up thy bed, and walk," declared the Master (Matthew 9:2; Mark 2:9). The man did as Jesus bid.

Among the many who witnessed this miracle were learned scribes of the Torah, men who prided themselves on their understanding of the legalities of Jewish law. They did not marvel with others over the miracle, but reasoned among themselves, "Why doth this man thus speak blasphemies? who can forgive sins but God only?" (Mark 2:7).

Those who watched the miraculous healing of this man were "amazed" (Mark 1:27). They said to one another, "What thing is this? what new doctrine is this?" (Mark 1:27). Amid their musings, they did not reject Jesus as those in Nazareth had done. Instead, they joyously shared their amazement with those not present in the synagogue that day, "and immediately his fame spread abroad throughout all the region round about Galilee" (Mark 1:28).

The name "Jesus of Nazareth" was heard by young and old in villages and along byways throughout Galilee. The sick and afflicted, upon learning of a miracle worker in Capernaum, came from every direction seeking Jesus, and he "healed all" (Matthew 8:16). Of those who suffered and

These hypocrites knew the law and believed themselves capable of exposing a blasphemer, but unwittingly they were self-righteously condemning the Son of God.

Jesus asked them, "Why reason ye these things in your hearts?" (Mark 2:8) Without waiting for their answer, he declared, "That ye may know that the Son of man hath power on earth to forgive sins," he then said to the palsied man, "Arise, and take up thy bed, and go thy way into thine house" (Mark 2:10-11). As the man followed counsel, many of those who remained in the home were "amazed, and glorified God" (Mark 2:12). They were heard to say, "We never saw it on this fashion" (Mark 2:12). They, like others who had witnessed a miracle, proclaimed the goodness and

mercy of Jesus. These witnesses, although a significant number, soon became small in comparison to the multitudes who would yet testify of the compassion of Jesus.

Some of those who would comprise these new multitudes were found along the shores of the Sea of Galilee, others in Judaea, and at least one, Matthew Levi, sitting at his custom office on the international road near Capernaum.[1] Each answered the call, "Follow me," and like other disciples—Andrew, Peter, Philip, and John—left their vocations and became followers of the Son of God (Matthew 9:9).

Jesus eventually left believer and unbeliever alike in Galilee for a brief season to once again go up to Jerusalem to attend the Feast of Passover. As he approached the end

Approximately 450 A.D., an octagonal stone church was built on the site where Christians believe Peter's house stood.

This limestone synagogue, the most prominent structure in Capernaum, was built in the fourth century on a first-century basalt foundation.

Today the people of Israel include Bedouins, Muslims, Jews, and Christians. Two Arab men converse in the ancient town of Jericho.

of his journey and the temple courts in the Holy City, he saw "a great multitude of impotent folk, of blind, halt, withered" near the twin pools of Bethesda (John 5:3).[2] Of particular notice was a man who had suffered from an infirmity for thirty-eight years. "Wilt thou be made whole?" Jesus asked. The impotent man responded, "I have no man, when the water is troubled, to put me into the pool: but while I am coming, another steppeth down before me" (John 5:6). His explanation reflected his belief in the Jewish superstition that an angel entered the pool of Bethesda and disturbed the water, giving momentary power to the water to heal the first person who entered. Jesus did not condone the superstition, but demonstrated his power over afflictions by stating, "Rise, take up thy bed, and walk" (John 5:8). Immediately the man arose, took his bed, and walked.

Many Jews, perhaps pilgrims who had come to Jerusalem for the Passover festivities, saw the man carrying his bed in the temple courts on that Sabbath day. They chided him, "It is not lawful for thee to carry thy bed" (John 5:10). He answered the hecklers, "He that made me whole, the same said unto me, Take up thy bed, and walk" (John 5:11). When asked to point to the man that had so advised him, Jesus "conveyed himself away" from the scene (John 5:13). Later, he found the man in the temple courts and said to him, "Behold, thou art made whole: sin no more, lest a worse thing come unto thee" (John 5:14). Whether the man sinned again is not known. What is known is that the man announced to one and all "that it was Jesus, which had made him whole" (John 5:15).

His words, perhaps spoken in innocence, led to vengeful persecutions against the Lord. "Blasphemy!" was the cry heard among the Pharisees. To them, Jesus had broken restrictive rules governing the Sabbath day. But even more discomforting to these Jewish leaders was his declaration that "God was his Father, making himself equal with God" (John 5:18).

Jesus answered these pharisaic charges with one of the most quoted sermons in the Gospels. Such verses as, "Search the scriptures; for in them ye think ye have eternal life: and they are they which testify of me" and "For had ye believed Moses, ye would have believed me: for he wrote of me. But if ye believe not his writings, how shall ye believe my words?" (John 5:39, 46-47) have been repeated with joy for millennia in Christian churches throughout the world.

But joy was not expressed by the Jewish leaders present on that occasion. They were angry, yet allowed Jesus to go his way among the Passover pilgrims unmolested. Nevertheless, he and his disciples did not pass unobserved. Pharisees seemed to be at his every turn. When Jesus walked "through the corn fields on the sabbath day," Pharisees observed his disciples plucking "the ears of corn" (Mark 2:23). "Why do they on the sabbath day that which is not lawful?" they asked (Mark 2:24). Jesus answered their question with a question of his own: "Have ye never read what David did?" (Mark 2:25). He then proceeded to remind the self-appointed guardians of Judaism about their favored King of Israel, David. Jesus told them of David and his men eating the sacred shewbread—bread placed in the presence of Jehovah symbolizing communion with God. Jesus then said, "The sabbath was made for man, and not man for the sabbath . . . For the Son of man is Lord even of the sabbath day" (Mark 2:27; Matthew 12:8).

Unable to refute his words, the Pharisees were left to wonder at his teachings; but still they followed him, surreptitiously hoping to entrap the Son of God. Inside a synagogue they asked, "Is it lawful to heal on the sabbath days?" (Matthew 12:10). Jesus replied by speaking of the absurdity of leaving a sheep in a pit on the Sabbath. Then, turning to

An Arab woman bargaining in one of the numerous marketplaces in the Old City.

Jewish man reciting prayers at the Western Wall.

a man afflicted with a withered hand, he said, "Stretch forth thine hand" (Matthew 12:13). As he did so, "it was restored whole, like as the other" (Matthew 12:13). Instead of rejoicing with the healed man, the Pharisees left the synagogue and held a private council on "how they might destroy [Jesus]" (Matthew 12:14). He was disturbing their definition of a true Israel, a pure Israel, a nation free from sinners, harlots, publicans, and Sabbath violators. They concluded that he must be destroyed to protect Israel— even if it meant aligning themselves with the Herodians, the most despised political sect in Judaea.

Rather than wait for their next entrapment, Jesus "withdrew himself" from the Holy City of Jerusalem

A devout Jewish man prays in a swaying motion at the Western Wall. He is wearing a prayer shawl or garment called a talith, which he moves from shoulder to shoulder during his prayer. In the cracks of the wall are pieces of paper. Written on the paper are prayers and the names of people for whom prayers are being said.

Interior of the Church of the Beatitudes.

(Matthew 12:15). "Great multitudes followed him, and he healed them all" (Matthew 12:15). He journeyed to the coasts of the cosmopolitan cities of Tyre and Sidon, and from there to the Sea of Galilee. From the sea he climbed a mountain, and in a level plateau on the mount he communed with God. After the communion, Jesus called and ordained twelve apostles—men who would be sent forth to proclaim his gospel.[3]

Seven of the twelve were mentioned in the Gospels before their call—Andrew, John, Simon Peter, Philip, Nathanael, James, and Levi Matthew. Eleven of the twelve were from Galilee, and only Judas, the Iscariot, was from Judah.

Jesus then "opened his mouth, and taught them" what has become known as the Sermon on the Mount (Matthew 5:2). His teachings that day were not merely a series of comments or speeches made at various locations and combined by the writer Matthew to appear as one sermon. These sayings, spoken on the mount to the chosen twelve, are beatitudes, for they beautify and outline the pathway to eternal happiness.

As the beatitudes are read again and again, our understanding of the apostles' call to preserve the power of the covenants between God and Israel, to share the gospel with others, and to glorify God is better understood. We learn of the twelve being taught of the symbolism of salt, bushels, candles, and lilies. We learn that although almsgiving was a public process devised to relieve the burdens of the poor throughout Judaea, alms from the twelve were to be given in secret, so that "thy Father which seeth in secret himself shall reward thee openly" (Matthew 6:4). We learn that when the twelve prayed to God, they were to "not be as the hypocrites," who faced Jerusalem with heads covered and eyes cast down, and recited prayers each morning, midday, and afternoon on street corners, in crowded marketplaces, and in synagogues (Matthew 6:5). Jesus admonished them to "enter into thy closet" (a small adjoining room or inner chamber attached to Jewish homes that contained the family's supplies and valuables) to pray (Matthew 6:6).

We also gain further insights into prayer with Jesus' reminder to his apostles that "when ye pray, use not vain repetitions, as the heathen do" (Matthew 6:7). For heathens, the number of prayers, not their sincerity, influenced the granting of a petition. Jesus decried the heathen's prayer as vain repetition, meaning the prayer had no value.

He then prayed, showing the chosen twelve the correct manner to pray. This glorious supplication, the Lord's

Prayer, has been uttered by generations of Christians in an effort to mirror their God. (See Matthew 6:9-13.)

Jesus next counseled his apostles to put aside material cares—to "consider the lilies of the field, how they grow; they toil not, neither do they spin: And yet I say unto you, That even Solomon in all his glory was not arrayed like one of these" (Matthew 6:28-29). Jesus wanted his chosen twelve to have faith. He warned them not to give "that which is holy unto the dogs, neither cast ye your pearls before swine"—the two animals that were despised by the Jews (Matthew 7:6)—but to "enter ye in at the strait gate . . . which leadeth unto life, and few there be that find it" (Matthew 7:13-14). The Master knew the gate and the way to happiness in this life and eternal perfection. Through his words, he now guided the twelve. "When Jesus had ended these sayings, the [apostles] were astonished at his doctrine: For he taught them as one having authority, and not as the scribes" (Matthew 7:28-29).

▲ On a hillside overlooking the Sea of Galilee, Jesus gave the Sermon on the Mount to his selected disciples.

◄ The Church of the Beatitudes is the traditional site where Jesus gave the Sermon on the Mount. From the site the cities of Safed and Tiberias are easily seen. Safed is likely the city referred to when Jesus said, "A city that is set on an hill cannot be hid" (Matthew 5:14).

CHAPTER 5

FROM THE VALLEY TO THE MOUNT

PHOTOGRAPHER'S NOTE - MAY 6, 1998
SEA OF GALILEE

It is early morning and still dark. According to Roman reckoning, it is the fourth watch. The birds in the trees are beginning to sing to a new day.

Spread before me is a panoramic view of the Sea of Galilee. Across the sea the lights of Tiberius and Safed glitter in the thick air that hangs over this legendary lake. Even in the dark blue haze, cities on a hill cannot be hid. As I gaze through this light, no longer night but not quite morning, I think of Jesus calming the wind and the sea. I wonder if it was on such a night as this that he walked on the water toward the boat where startled disciples rowed against the wind. He called to them, "Shalom, Shalom Aleichem," interpreted as "Be of good cheer." He then bid Peter to walk with him.

Jesus left the Mount of Beatitudes and its solitude, where he had ordained his apostles and taught them the pathway to eternal life, to continue his ministry along the busy byways and paths of Galilee. As he again went from village to village, he extended compassion to those whose lives knew sorrow—the widow, the centurion, Jarius, and thousands gathered on the plains of Bethsaida. Each was blessed, and each knew of his mercy.

In the Jezreel Valley, "when he came nigh to the gate of the city" of Nain, he witnessed a large funeral procession (Luke 7:12). The woman who caught the attention of Jesus that day was a widow, and the dead her only son. At some point in the procession, Jesus "had compassion" on the widowed mother and said to her, "Weep not" (Luke 7:13). He then "touched the bier," and as he did so, those who were carrying it "stood still" (Luke 7:14). "Young man, I say unto thee, Arise," Jesus said. The young man "sat up, and began to speak" (Luke 7:15). Witnesses of this miracle were fearful, yet glorified God. "A great prophet is risen up among us," some exclaimed, while others mused, "God hath visited his people" (Luke 7:16). The wonder and greatness of this miracle was told to "all of Judaea, and the region round about" (Luke 7:17).

◄ *"And in the fourth watch of the night [between three and six o'clock in the morning] Jesus went unto them, walking on the sea" (Matthew 14:25).*

◄ *(opposite page) A huge rock escarpment rises from the ruins of Caesarea Philippi. Jesus was near this site when he asked Peter, "Whom do men say that I the Son of man am?" (Matthew 15:13). Peter replied, "Thou art the Christ, the Son of the living God" (Matthew 16:16).*

The fertile Jezreel Valley lies between the hills of Nazareth and the city of Nain. Once a malaria-infested swamp, it is now the breadbasket of Israel.

Bethesda means "house of mercy" or "house of grace." "Now there is at Jerusalem by the sheep market a pool, which is called in the Hebrew tongue Bethesda, having five porches" (John 5:2). It was here that Jesus healed an invalid on the Sabbath, which raised criticism from the Jewish leaders.

Perhaps the centurion of Capernaum, the Roman soldier who had built a synagogue, was among those who heard of the healing power of Jesus of Nazareth. For "when Jesus was entered into Capernaum, there came unto him a centurion," a man with responsibility for an infantry unit of fifty to a hundred soldiers (Matthew 8:5). The centurion addressed Jesus as "Lord," evidencing his faith that the man he approached was more than a mere miracle worker (Matthew 8:6). He then expressed concern for another, rather than asking a blessing for himself as one might expect from a Roman soldier assigned to protect land governed by Herod Antipas. "My servant lieth at home sick of the palsy, grievously tormented," he told Jesus (Matthew 8:6).

His statement was a request for Jesus to heal the ailing servant. His request was most unusual. Roman soldiers, many of whom were recruited from among the Samaritans and Gentiles of Caesarea, were notorious for their unkindness to servants and slaves during the days of Jesus. If the centurion was actually asking the Lord to heal his servant, he was more enlightened than the Greco-Roman society in which he lived. Even so, before we grant him undue social enlightenment, a momentary review of the literal translation of the biblical passage reveals that it should read, "my [boy] lieth at home sick of the palsy, grievously tormented" (Matthew 8:6).

Whether we accept the literal or traditional translation of the Matthew or Luke account, there is no question that Jesus had compassion on the centurion and recognized his faith. "I will come and heal him," said Jesus (Matthew 8:7). The centurion answered, "Lord, I am not worthy that thou shouldest come under my roof: but speak the word only, and my servant shall be healed" (Matthew 8:8). The faith of this soldier led Jesus to say to the gathered descendants of the House of Israel in Capernaum, "Verily I say unto you, I have

Loaves of freshly baked bread are sold in the markets of Jerusalem.

Wheat continues to be harvested in Israel today.

the listener's response to the kingdom of God. (See Luke 8:5-8, 13-15; Mark 4:5, 8, 16.) Jesus concluded the parable by saying, "Who hath ears to hear, let him hear. Take heed what ye hear . . . and unto you that hear shall more be given" (Matthew 13:9; Mark 4:24).

Although his reference to hearing and ears sounds confusing to Western listeners, it was understood by the multitude. A common scene in Jewish schools was a rabbi whispering into an interpreter's ear the words he wanted his students to hear. The interpreter, who heard the rabbi's message in Hebrew, proclaimed aloud in Aramaic what the rabbi had said. If the interpreter added words or took away any words whispered by the rabbi, he was subject to dismissal. Likewise, those who heard the parable of the sower were to proclaim to all people what Jesus had said.

The apostles, as special witnesses for Jesus Christ, were to proclaim not only the words of the parable, but "to know the mysteries of the kingdom of heaven," and to testify of these mysteries from the housetops and from city to city, much like the man who ascended the pinnacle of the temple and announced the arrival of the Sabbath (Matthew 13:11). The apostles were not to be as the sleepy farmer, whose fields were overcome with tares by his own neglect. They were to testify to all that the kingdom of God was upon the earth. The kingdom was likened unto a grain of a mustard seed, which has a small beginning, but when nourished grows into a large, attractive plant. (See Matthew 13:31; Mark 4:30-31.)

To the follower who offered an excuse for his reluctance to proclaim the gospel—"Suffer me first to go and bury my father"—Jesus said, "Let the dead bury their dead" (Matthew 8:21-22).[1] He then explained, "No man, having put his hand to the plough, and looking back, is fit for the kingdom of God" (Luke 9:62). Jesus knew that looking back

▲ (top) Fields of golden grain are seen near Bet Shemish (the village of Samson) and the Valley of Elah (made famous when young David slew Goliath).

▲ Sheefa, a widow, holds mustard seeds picked from her own tree in Bethany.

▶ Mustard blossoms produce seeds the size of small grains of sand.

▶ (opposite page) Pods of mustard seeds are gathered and dried in large bowls.

not found so great faith, no, not in Israel" (Matthew 8:10). Then, turning to the centurion, he said, "Go thy way; and as thou hast believed, so be it done unto thee" (Matthew 8:13). The afflicted, who was dear to the centurion, enjoyed a healing blessing from that very hour.

Some time later, Jesus went down to the Sea of Galilee, where he entered a ship. A multitude gathered along the shoreline to listen as he spoke in parables of the kingdom of God. (See Matthew 13:3.) In the parable of the sower, Jesus portrayed the seed as good, as are all things pertaining to the kingdom of God. The variable was the type of soil the seed fell upon—good soil, stony portions of land, on the roadway, and under thick vegetation. The soil represented resulted in uneven furrows for the farmer. Likewise, the follower who used life's circumstances as an excuse for not sharing the good news of the kingdom was unsteady in his commitment to the Lord. "My mother and my brethren are these which hear the word of God, and do it," said the Master (Luke 8:21).

Jesus then sailed across the Sea of Galilee with those disciples who were steady in their resolve to seek first the kingdom of God. During their voyage, the Lord slept. Suddenly, the placid waters of Galilee turned from calm to rough squalls caused by an easternly wind. Water began to fill the ship, and all aboard seemed in jeopardy from the soaring waves. "Master, master, we perish," shouted the fearful disciples (Luke 8:24). The awakened Master knew such was not to be. These men had accepted his teachings and would yet know greater service. For their sake, Jesus arose and "rebuked the wind and the raging of the water: and they ceased" (Luke 8:24). No longer did it appear that Galilee, sweet Galilee, was like the high seas. The Master had spoken, and the winds and the sea obeyed his voice.

They continued their voyage in safety and reached the east side of Galilee, the country of the Gadarenes. Among the first to see Jesus disembark from the ship was a man who lived outside the city limits among the tombs. In haste he came to the Lord, crying out with a loud voice, "What have I to do with thee, Jesus, thou Son of the most high God? I adjure thee by God, that thou torment me not" (Mark 5:7). "What is thy name?" Jesus asked (Mark 5:9). The unclean man answered, "My name is Legion: for we are many" (Mark 5:9). Jesus commanded, "Come out of the man, thou unclean spirit" (Mark 5:8).

The spirit left the man and entered a herd of two thousand swine feeding on the mountain slopes nearby. Possessed by evil spirits, the swine were uncontrollable.

They "ran violently down a steep place into the sea, . . . and were choked" (Mark 5:13). The dramatic loss of the swine evoked fear in the men responsible for their care. We assume these men were not Jews, but Gentiles. The assumption is based on the name of the Roman military unit stationed in the area—legion, and the insignia of the unit—a boar.

The men hurried into the nearby city and reported the unusual events at the seashore. Many who heard their account of the drowning of the swine came to the shore to see for themselves. It was not the carcasses of the swine that caused them to fear, but the crazed man, who lived among the tombs, seated next to Jesus "clothed, and in his right mind" (Mark 5:15). Their fear led them to ask Jesus to leave Gadarenes. He did leave the region, but not without leaving a vivid reminder of his compassion. "Go home to thy friends, and tell them how great things the Lord hath done for thee," he told the healed man (Mark 5:19). The man did as he was told, and "all men did marvel" (Mark 5:20).

Jesus again entered the ship and sailed to the other side of the sea. There many people crowded him, wanting relief from their sorrows and cares of life. Among their number was Jarius, the ruler of a local synagogue, whose "daughter lieth at the point of death" (Mark 5:23). Jesus agreed to follow Jarius to his home, where his daughter lay. As he walked toward the home, many of life's unfortunate pressed against him, including a woman suffering from an issue of blood. Although treated by physicians, her twelve-year illness had not abated. Hoping that "If I may touch but his clothes, I shall be whole," she pushed herself forward and clung to the Master's garment for a brief moment (Mark 5:28).[2]

"Who touched my clothes?" Jesus asked, sensing that "virtue had gone out of him" (Mark 5:30). Although the disciples assured him that many had touched his clothing, only the woman could respond to his query. She fell down before her Lord and told him of the circumstances that caused her to approach him. (See Mark 5:33.) "Daughter, thy faith hath made thee whole; go in peace, and be whole of thy plague," said Jesus (Mark 5:34).

As he neared the home of Jarius, a messenger attempted to arrest his steps. "Thy daughter is dead," he told Jarius and then asked, "Why troublest thou the Master any further?" (Mark 5:35). Yet Jesus and Jarius proceeded to the home, in which weeping and wailing for the lost daughter pierced the air. By the Master's touch to her hand and the words, "Damsel, I say unto thee, arise," the twelve-year-old girl arose and walked (Mark 5:41).

This glorious miracle, with others yet to come, was in vivid contrast to the rumors spreading through Galilee of the brutal death of John the Baptist. Tales of the licentious dancing of Salome and her foolish abandonment of the sacred, and rumors of Herodias' ordering the "headless trunk [of John the Baptist] to be flung out over the battlements for dogs and vultures to devour," angered Galileans.[3] They decried the execution of John without a trial and the manner of his demise. Seeing no other recourse than war, Galileans threatened insurrection against Rome and its appointees to avenge the death of John.

With Galilean swords pointed toward Herod Antipas, it was no longer safe for Jesus to walk the shores of Galilee. He departed into a "desert place apart"—the secluded area of Bethsaida-Julias. There he was safe from Herod Antipas, who fantasized that Jesus was John the Baptist risen from the dead and "desired to see him" (Luke 9:9). He was also safe from the Roman appointee Pontias Pilate, who had killed Galilean pilgrims threatening rebellion. By retreating to Bethsaida, Jesus was in a land ruled by Philipp, and momentarily out of harm's way.

(opposite page) Grain fields still adorn the countryside near the site where Jesus fed the multitudes at Bethsaida.

The Franciscan Basilica of the Transfiguration on Mount Tabor was built between 1921-1923. The Basilica is near the ruins of older Druze and Crusader structures, and the Tomb of Melchizedek.

Mount Tabor, located near Nazareth in the Jezreel Valley, is the traditional site where Jesus was transfigured.

▲ *A poor beggar reaches for assistance. Crowds in the street merely ignore his hand and walk past.*

▼ *"Behold a bright cloud overshadowed them: and behold a voice out of the cloud, which said, This is my beloved Son, in whom I am well pleased; hear ye him" (Matthew 17:5). Light rays shining through the clouds above Mount Tabor.*

When disciples of Jesus learned that he no longer walked the shores of Galilee, they followed him out of the cities to the plains of Bethsaida. He was their hope for a better world—a world free from insurrection, strife, and pain. They wanted to be near him. When closer disciples suggested that he send them away as evening approached, Jesus would not. With only a simple peasant meal of fishes and barley loaves, Jesus fed thousands seated in companies and ranks of fifties and hundreds in the grassy meadow of Bethsaida. As they ate their barley bread and opsarion, reminiscent of the goodness of Jehovah in providing manna for the fleeing Israelites, they did not know Jesus was signaling his advent. "Whom say the people that I am?" Jesus asked (Luke 9:18). He was answered, "John the Baptist; but some say, Elias; and others say, that one of the old prophets is risen again" (Luke 9:19). The multitude did not know that the man who provided manna was the promised Messiah, yet they did know they wanted to crown him king of Judaea. (See John 6:15.)

Jesus did not want the honors of men, and commanded his disciples to leave the grassy meadow of Bethsaida, enter a boat, and cross the Sea of Galilee. They obeyed. "And when he had sent them away," Jesus departed from the multitude "into a mountain to pray" (Mark 6:46). After communing with God, he joined his disciples, who were rowing against a contrary wind sweeping the sea. They had "rowed about five and twenty or thirty furlongs" (about three or four miles from the shore) by the fourth watch of the night (sometime between three and six in the morning), when in the early rays of dawn they saw Jesus "walking upon the sea" (John 6:19; Mark 6:47). The wind ceased as he came to the ship, and the disciples were "sore amazed" (Mark 6:51).

Their amazement didn't cease as they reached the shore, and again Jesus entered the villages dotting Galilee. He healed all manner of diseases within the villages, and "as many as touched him were made whole" (Mark 6:56). It seemed that nothing would disrupt the healing ministry of Jesus—not element, not water, and certainly not those blessed by his hand.

Yet it was the very ones who had partaken of his compassion who turned against him—the turncoats within the multitude who had eaten of the miraculous manna in Bethsaida. When they discovered that Jesus had left the meadow, they went searching for him and found him in Capernaum, preaching in the synagogue. "I am the bread of life: he that cometh to me shall never hunger; and he that believeth on me shall never thirst," said Jesus (John 6:35). His words were not well received by those who wanted literal bread.

The antagonistic response to the Bread of Life sermon marked the first time that popular opinion of Jesus waned. "Those who had hoped to find a . . . political leader in Him saw their dreams melt away: those who had no true sympathy for His life and words had an excuse for leaving Him," wrote scholar Cunningham Geikie. "Outward glory and material wealth were the national dream: he spoke only of inward purity."[4] The rend created that day was never mended.

He next journeyed to the pagan cities of Tyre and Sidon, where it might be supposed that the fame of Jesus had not yet reached.[5] But even in those Gentile lands, people had heard of him. "Have mercy on me, O Lord, thou Son of David; my daughter is grievously vexed with a devil," said a Canaanite woman (Matthew 15:22). Jesus answered the woman, "I am not sent but unto the lost sheep of the house of Israel" (Matthew 15:24). She was not to be thwarted in her quest, even when Jesus said, "It is not meet to take the children's bread, and to cast it to dogs" (Matthew 15:26). She retorted, "Truth, Lord: yet the dogs eat of the crumbs which fall from their masters' table" (Matthew 15:27). "O woman, great is thy faith: be it unto thee even as thou wilt," said Jesus. "And her daughter was made whole from that very hour" (Matthew 15:28).

Others also found relief from their sorrows, and as we might expect, thousands of Gentiles desired to be near Jesus. And then, almost in repetition of the miracle in Bethsaida, Jesus, with seven loaves and a few fishes, fed four thousand who had followed him for "three days, and have nothing to eat" (Matthew 15:32). And "they did all eat, and were filled" (Matthew 15:37). After this miraculous event, there was no attempt to make Jesus a temporal king, nor was there a division among his followers.

Jesus left the spiritually fed to once again return to Galilee. With a clear vision of his destiny, he knew he was returning to his ever-present antagonists. In the coasts of Magdala, Pharisees and Sadducees wanted him to show them a sign from heaven. (See Matthew 16:1.) Instead of the sign they sought, Jesus spoke of weather, a subject Jewish leaders knew well. They knew that lightning, storm clouds, and rain came from the west, and that snow mixed with hail was a rare occurrence. They were aware of seismic disturbances running north and south along the Rift Valley and that a red sky at night meant fair weather, etc. Jesus contrasted their ability to recognize the signs of nature with their inability to see the hand of God. "O ye hypocrites, ye can discern the face of the sky; but can ye not discern the signs of the times?" he asked (Matthew 16:3).

These naysayers did not see the greatest sign from heaven—the Son of God standing before them. They, like many of the Jews, failed to recognize Jesus as the Christ. But Peter knew him: "Thou art the Christ, the Son of the living God" (Matthew 16:16). Peter was privileged, along with apostles James and John, to see Jesus in his glorified, transfigured state.[6] They saw the face of our Lord "shine as the sun, and his raiment was white as the light" (Matthew 17:2). They witnessed the coming of the ancient prophets Moses and Elias, and received keys and authority from them. (See Matthew 17:1-13.) They were overshadowed by a bright cloud, "not a watery cloud, but what the Jews called the Shekinah or Dwelling cloud, the cloud which manifested the presence and glory of God."[7] They heard a voice from heaven say, "This is my beloved Son, in whom I am well pleased; hear ye him" (Matthew 17:5). The reaction of Peter, James, and John to witnessing these glorious visionary events was to fall on the ground and to be "sore afraid" (Matthew 17:6). It was the glorified Son of God who calmed their fears. "Arise, and be not afraid," said Jesus. "And when they had lifted up their eyes, they saw no man, save Jesus only" (Matthew 17:8).

The Mediterranean Sea as photographed from Caesarea.

CHAPTER 6

GALILEAN MINISTRY ENDS

The burial chamber located inside the Tomb of Lazarus.

(opposite page) An Arab man is kissed by his camel. For a few shekels, he will allow his camel to kiss tourists.

PHOTOGRAPHER'S NOTE - APRIL 27, 1998
BETHANY

On a short walk on a narrow street up a hill, Arab hawkers thrust cheap postcards, bookmarks, water, and an assortment of other contemporary trinkets in my face. "One dolla! Two dolla!" they yell. A few just hold out an empty hand, asking for money. A small shop and crude signs boast of Lazarus souvenirs. One sign points to a doorway, a cave-like opening leading down rock steps—"Lazarus Tomb."

I read with others the account in John, chapter eleven, but we are interrupted by pilgrims coming and going, cars passing on the narrow street, honking as they maneuver through the crowd waiting to enter the tomb.

The chamber of the tomb will only accommodate a small group of people, so we take turns descending the stone steps leading down a tunnel cut in the limestone. "We have to hurry," we are told. "Others are waiting," we are reminded. "Hurry!"

I make my way down the steps to the weeping chamber, then on hands and knees I crawl backward into the burial chamber.

Click, click, a couple of pictures, and then back up the stairs to the brightness of daylight.

Outside again, waiting for others to have their turn, I sit on the rocks and try, just for a moment, to think about this place and what happened here. The shortest verse in the New Testament, "Jesus wept," was written about this place (John 11:35). A beloved friend had lain dead for four days. Mary and Martha wept and mourned the loss of their brother, Lazarus. Others with them also wept. Jesus, seeing the grief in the eyes and faces of dear friends, requested that the stone sealing the tomb be removed, and then "cried in a loud voice, Lazarus, come forth. And he that was dead came forth" (John 11:43-44).

I was separated from the now—from the noise, the people, and the souvenirs. A chill went down my spine and tears filled my eyes. This is where it happened.

Jesus descended from the lofty heights to once again minister to the people living along the byways of Galilee. The afflicted sought him at every turn.

☙ ▲ *Saint Peter's Fish is served in restaurants in Tiberias. A few fortunate customers receive a fish with a shekel coin in its mouth, reminiscent of the fish Peter caught to pay the tribute money. (Matthew 17:24-27)*

☙ ▶ *Bedouin children rush from their camps to greet the tourists.*

The situation of the man whose lunatic son had been blessed by the disciples, yet remained tormented, became a teaching moment for Jesus. "O faithless and perverse generation," said the Master to his disciples, "how long shall I be with you? how long shall I suffer you? bring him hither to me" (Matthew 17:17). The child was cured of his malady by the Lord. The disciples, witnessing the miraculous healing, asked, "Why could not we cast him out?" (Matthew 17:19). Jesus taught them the importance of faith, prayer, and fasting in the healing process.

These eternal concepts were reinforced as the disciples walked daily with Jesus from one seaside village to another. So in step did they become with the truths of eternity, that it must have been surprising when Peter was approached in Capernaum about a temporal matter. "Doth not your master pay tribute?" he was asked (Matthew 17:24). The question dealt with tribute monies collected in the name of Caesar throughout provinces in the Roman Empire. For decades, Jewish rabbis had been exempt from paying tribute to the Roman overlords. Because Jesus had never received the formal training necessary to become a rabbi, yet multitudes recognized him as a great teacher, the question was not without merit. Jesus, overhearing the query, told Peter, "Lest we should offend them," meaning the publicans who collected tribute for Rome, "go thou to the sea, and cast an hook, and take up the fish that first cometh up; and when thou hast opened his mouth, thou shalt find a piece of money" (Matthew 17:27).[1] Peter did as the Lord directed and found the coin. The coin was then given as tribute not only for Jesus, the great teacher, but Peter, the obedient disciple.

Following the temporal offering, when Peter was reminded of the greatness of the wealth and power of Rome, the disciples wondered aloud, "Who is the greatest in the kingdom of heaven?" (Matthew 18:1). The answer given by

Jesus was in juxtaposition to the public adulation demanded by the Roman emperor; he admonished his disciples to become as a child. "Except ye be converted, and become as little children, ye shall not enter the kingdom of heaven," he said (Matthew 18:3). For the disciple who longed to be the greatest in that kingdom, Jesus prescribed attaining the humility of a "little child" (Matthew 18:4).

To ensure that his followers aspired to humility and innocence, Jesus advised them to "despise not one of these little" children or cause them to falter in their faithfulness (Matthew 18:10). For such offenses against a child, Jesus observed that "it were better for [the offender] that a millstone were hanged about his neck, and that he were drowned in the depth of the sea" (Matthew 18:6). This form of death, used by the Romans in Galilee for crimes of peculiar enormity, was repugnant to the Jews.[2]

Peter had questions about forgiveness, even for such grave crimes. "Lord, how oft shall my brother sin against me, and I forgive him?" he asked (Matthew 18:21). In the days of Jesus, rabbis counseled that three offenses were to be pardoned, but no more. Jesus said to Peter, "Until seventy times seven," metaphorically expanding forgiveness to infinity (Matthew 18:22). Jesus was counseling Peter to recognize that even though the magnitude of the offense was enormous, forgiveness was the appropriate action. It may not have been coincidental that soon after equating forgiveness with infinity, Jesus appointed seventy men to go "two and two before his face into every city and place, whither he himself would come" (Luke 10:1).

As the seventy proclaimed the good news of the kingdom in cities and villages of Galilee and Judaea, Jesus took another road. He turned aside from the familiar paths of Galilee and went to Jerusalem, the Holy City. The annual Feast of Tabernacles held in the city beckoned him, as it had

pilgrims for centuries. (See Exodus 23:16.) Pilgrims enjoyed the spirit of thanksgiving present in the festivities. "It is better to spend one day in God's courts [on the Temple Mount] than a thousand days elsewhere," weary pilgrims claimed.[3]

Although many of the travelers stayed in Jerusalem, Jesus lodged in the village of Bethany, a short distance from the Holy City. His abode, a temporary booth made of boughs, was constructed near the home of Mary and Martha.[4] The booth, like hundreds of other booths erected throughout Jerusalem, was a reminder of the makeshift abodes of ancient Israelites as they wandered in the wilderness.

It is not known whether Jesus participated in the public sacrifices offered on the Temple Mount during the Feast

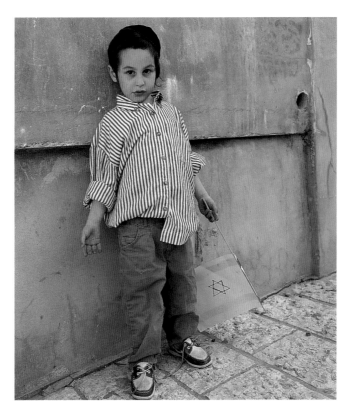

The Good Samaritan Inn on the Jericho road is a reminder of the answer Jesus gave to the question, "And who is my neighbour?" (Luke 10:29).

A young Jewish boy holds his homemade flag to celebrate the fiftieth anniversary of Israeli independence.

A blind man begging for coins outside the Church of the Annunciation.

Unattended goats and sheep roam free in the Judaean wilderness. Once a year on Yom Kippur, the Day of Atonement, an unblemished goat was taken from Jerusalem out the Gate Beautiful. Symbolically, the goat was burdened with the sins of Israel and was known as a scapegoat.

of the Tabernacles or whether he watched the ceremonial rituals that required the services of "not fewer than 446 priests and an equal number of Levites."[5] If he had been in attendance, he would have witnessed throngs of worshipers waving palm branches as an appointed Levite walked to the pool of Siloam to draw water. When two pints were drawn from the pool, the Levite pronounced that he had living water and poured the water into a golden ewer, which he carried to the temple altar. When the living water was poured into a silver basin near the altar, the chant of Hallel began. (See Psalm 113-118.) During the chant, those who waved palm branches exclaimed, "Praise ye the Lord" (Psalm 117:2).

At or near these climactic moments, Jesus beckoned, "Come unto me" (John 7:37). "If any man thirst, let him come unto me, and drink. He that believeth on me, as the scripture hath said, out of his belly shall flow rivers of living water" (John 7:37-38). As the multitude listened to his words, which were symbolic of the living water at the temple altar, some said aloud, "Of a truth this is the Prophet" (John 7:40). Others said, "This is the Christ" (John 7:41). Even those in the employ of the chief priests and Pharisees cried, "Never man spake like this man" (John 7:46).

His words were prophetic and his doctrine true. Yet scribes and Pharisees refused to accept him as the Christ or as a prophet. They challenged his wisdom, authority, and

trary to the Mosaic law. By stating, "He that is without sin among you, let him first cast a stone," the heavy yoke of legal entanglements presented by the scribes and Pharisees was avoided (John 8:7).[7]

A lawyer next stepped forward to tempt Jesus to judge amiss. "Master, what shall I do to inherit eternal life?" he asked (Luke 10:25). Jesus asked him, "What is written in the law?" (Luke 10:26). "Thou shalt love the Lord thy God with all thy heart, and with all thy soul, and with all thy strength, and with all thy mind; and thy neighbour as thyself," replied the lawyer (Luke 10:27). Then pointedly he asked Jesus, "And who is my neighbour?" (Luke 10:29). Jesus answered with the parable of the Good Samaritan, challenging the restrictive Jewish definition of a neighbor. "[Who] was neighbour unto him that fell among the thieves?," Jesus asked the lawyer (Luke 10:36). The lawyer answered, "He that shewed mercy on him" (Luke 10:37). Jesus then said, "Go and do thou likewise" (Luke 10:37).

In due course, like the Good Samaritan, Jesus left his followers for a season. This time it was the wintry Feast of Dedication, known as Hanukkah, that beckoned him to Jerusalem. (See John 10:22.) Although Hanukkah was not one of the great feasts celebrated in the Holy City, it was a favorite feast—a time to express national rejoicing and receive a forgiveness of past wrongs.

Differing from these festivities was the Day of Atonement, a day of fasting. On this day a scapegoat, symbolically burdened with the sins of Israel, was led out the eastern gate of the Holy City to the Mount of Olives, and from there into the wilderness by a temple priest. (See Leviticus 16:21-22.) Once the goat was in the wilderness, all the sins of Israel were believed to have vanished.

With the pilgrims' thoughts turned to the scapegoat, so symbolic of the Savior-Deliverer, it is no wonder that those

▲ A young man in the Old City of Jerusalem wearing items of clothing from multiple cultures.

◄ The steep hillsides, where the Kidron Valley and Hinnom Valley or Valley of Gehenna meet, are known as the City of David.

▼ The Church of Saint Lazarus in Bethany.

knowledge again and again, hoping to find fault. On one occasion they even brought before Jesus "a woman taken in adultery," hoping to entangle him in a legal foray between the law of Moses and the rule of Rome (John 8:3). "Master," they asked, "Now Moses in the law commanded us, that such should be stoned: but what sayest thou?" (John 8:5). These men knew that under Roman rule, Jews inflicting the death penalty were frowned upon. They also knew that even though the law of Moses "decreed death by stoning as the penalty for adultery," such punishment had ended centuries before.[6] If Jesus concluded the woman should suffer death by stoning, he would defy Roman law. If he concluded she should not suffer death, his decision would be con-

The entrance to the Tomb of Lazarus.

The weeping chamber located inside the Tomb of Lazarus.

who thronged around Jesus on this occasion asked, "How long dost thou make us to doubt? If thou be the Christ, tell us plainly" (John 10:24). Jesus answered, "I told you, and ye believed not: the works that I do in my Father's name, they bear witness of me. . . . I and my Father are one" (John 10:25, 30). Instead of accepting his answer and worshiping him, his inquisitors "took up stones again to stone him," claiming that "for a good work we stone thee not; but for blasphemy, and because that thou, being a man, makest thyself God" (John 10:31, 33).

Jesus escaped death by stoning and other evil designs contrived by his enemies. He left Jerusalem and the naysayers, and went "beyond Jordan into the place where John at first baptized; and there he abode" (John 10:40). In this wilderness setting, he concluded his healing ministry. He had come full circle since his baptism in the area years before. Many of those he ministered among remembered the testimony of John and said, "John did no miracle: but all things that John spake of this man were true" (John 10:41).

Jesus did not remain long in the serene setting of fond memories among believers. Some claim a Pharisee's warning, "Get thee out, and depart hence: for Herod will kill thee" (Luke 13:31) was the reason. But not so. Jesus would leave the wilderness to fulfill the law of righteousness—the path laden with agonies and a cross.

As he anticipated Gethsemane and his ultimate sacrifice, the Lord uttered a series of parables—the wedding guests (Luke 14:7-11); the great supper (Luke 14:12-24); the lost sheep (Matthew 18:11-14); the lost coin (Luke 15:8-10); the prodigal son (Luke 15:11-32); the unjust steward, (Luke 16:1-13); Lazarus and the rich man (Luke 16:19-31); and the unprofitable servant (Luke 17:7-10).

The parable of the lost sheep, spoken at least twice by Jesus—once in Capernaum and again in the wilderness of

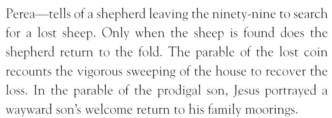

Perea—tells of a shepherd leaving the ninety-nine to search for a lost sheep. Only when the sheep is found does the shepherd return to the fold. The parable of the lost coin recounts the vigorous sweeping of the house to recover the loss. In the parable of the prodigal son, Jesus portrayed a wayward son's welcome return to his family moorings.

Many in the wilderness believed on Jesus, though only a few understood the underlying symbolism of the spoken parables. Yet each knew of the compassion of Jesus. It was this compassion, coupled with a knowledge of his own destiny, that led Jesus to leave the wilderness of Perea. Mary and Martha, his friends in Bethany, sent word to him that their brother Lazarus was numbered among the sick. "This sick-

◀ A small doorway in the large city gates of Jerusalem. A seventeenth-century tradition speaks of a "needle gate" being left open at night to allow people to pass in and out of the city, but not large caravans.

▲ (top) Although identified as the tree that Zacchaeus climbed to see Jesus, this tree is less than eight hundred years old.

▲ Camels are for hire at Tel Jericho, a favorite tourist stop in Israel.

▶ *A watchtower photographed at sunset in a canyon near Jerusalem.*

▼ *Burial cavities in a large, weathered-out boulder. Stone caskets were placed inside these cavities.*

ness is not unto death," said Jesus, "but for the glory of God, that the Son of God might be glorified thereby" (John 11:4).

Two days after receiving word of his friend's affliction, Jesus said to his disciples, "Let us go into Judaea again" (John 11:7). Although his disciples had heard the parables, they questioned his decision to go to Bethany, located so near Jerusalem. "Master, the Jews of late sought to stone thee; and goest thou thither again?" they asked (John 11:8). His reference to Lazarus' sleeping confused the disciples. It was not until he said, "Lazarus is dead . . . let us go unto him" that they understood why Jesus would risk his life to journey to Bethany (John 11:14-15). With courage, knowing something of the persecution that awaited all of them in Judaea, the apostle Thomas said, "Let us also go, that we may die with him" (John 11:16).[8]

By the time Jesus and his devoted disciples had arrived in Bethany, Lazarus "had lain in the grave four days already" (John 11:17). Noisy lamentations from bereaved family members and hired mourners, accompanied by flutes, pipes, and other musical instruments, would still be filling the air near the family home. Chairs and couches in the home would still be turned over and mourners seated on low stools, wearing torn garments as a sign of their sorrow.

Martha was the first to learn that "Jesus was coming," and left the home to meet him (John 11:20). Her greeting was one of remorse and pleading: "Lord, if thou hadst been here, my brother had not died. But I know, that even now, whatsoever thou wilt ask of God, God will give it thee" (John 11:21-22). Although Martha spoke of her faith in the "resurrection at the last day," Jesus spoke of the present when he declared, "Thy brother shall rise again" (John 11:23-24). The Lord was escorted to the grave site, where Lazarus had been laid—"a cave, and a stone lay upon it" (John 11:38). He asked that the stone be removed. After communing with his Father in Heaven, the Son of Man with a loud voice commanded, "Lazarus, come forth" (John 11:43). The dead arose, "bound hand and foot with graveclothes: and his face was bound about with a napkin" (John 11:44). "Loose him, and let him go," Jesus said, and it was done (John 11:44).

The miracle of raising Lazarus from the dead caused many who had vacillated about the identity of Jesus to believe on him. So many were convinced that Jesus was the Son of God that Jewish leaders were fearful of an uprising among the masses. They concluded that the people were being seduced by the miracles of Jesus and would rebel against Roman rule if he was not stopped. Rebellion against Rome would lead to a military display of might and bloody conflict in the streets of the Holy City. Power and concern for public order dominated their council that day. It was the high priest Joseph Caiaphas who had the answer: "It is expedient for us, that one man should die for the people, and that the whole nation perish not" (John 11:50). And "from that day forth" the Jewish leaders in Jerusalem counseled "together for to put [Jesus] to death" (John 11:53).

To avoid their plots, the Son of Man "walked no more openly among the Jews" (John 11:54). He left the mounting malice in Judaea and went to Ephraim, an isolated hillside town about twelve miles northeast of the Holy City, and from there to the coasts of Judaea beyond Jordan. (See John 11:54.) His teachings along the route, like the parables of the unjust judge and the Pharisee and the publican, are poignant reminders of the unrighteous judgment and pride of those who took counsel against him and plotted to destroy the very king they worshiped. (See Luke 18:1-14.)

Jesus now asked his apostles to accompany him as he concluded his ministry. "Behold, we go up to Jerusalem," he said (Matthew 20:18). "The Son of man shall be betrayed

The archeological dig at Jericho, known as Tel Jericho, has unearthed twenty-three occupational levels, including a neolithic town that existed nine thousand years ago.

unto the chief priests and unto the scribes, and they shall condemn him to death. And shall deliver him to the Gentiles to mock, and to scourge, and to crucify him: and the third day he shall rise again . . . the Son of man came not to be ministered unto, but to minister, and to give his life a ransom for many" (Matthew 20:18-19, 28).

Jesus and his chosen twelve turned once again toward Jerusalem. Along the route they passed through Jericho, and the Master healed the blind man who cried out, "Have mercy on us, O Lord, thou Son of David" (Matthew 20:30). He took notice of Zacchaeus, a man of small stature who had climbed a sycamore tree to see the Lord, and said unto him, "This day is salvation come to this house, forsomuch as he also is a son of Abraham. For the Son of man is come to seek and to save that which was lost" (Luke 19:9-10). He uttered the parable of the pounds and concluded with "those mine enemies, which would not that I should reign over them, bring hither, and slay them before me" (Luke 19:27). Thereafter, "he went before, ascending up to Jerusalem" (Luke 19:28).

CHAPTER 7

UP TO JERUSALEM

PHOTOGRAPHER'S NOTE - APRIL 25, 1998
GETHSEMANE

I sit in a grove of trees high on the Mount of Olives in quiet contemplation and read the scriptural passages of the suffering and personal sacrifice of Jesus Christ. A flood of emotion comes over me. As I read, I move closer to a nearby olive tree so I can touch it. I move again to a cluster of trees with branches that seem to reach out like open arms. I then stand amid the trees, stroking the branches at first and then leaning my head against the roughness of the bark. A sudden feeling of being in the embrace of Him who suffered for my sins comes over me. I feel the warmth of His love.

Moments later, I slowly walk down the Mount of Olives toward the Holy City along a path that Jesus may have followed. My daughter Lori is on one side of me, my wife Valerie and daughter Leslie on the other. With arms interlocked around each other, we descend the steep path. No words are spoken, but tears flow freely down our cheeks.

The last week of the Lord's mortal life, a subject that occupies more than a third of the Gospel narrative, began in the village of Bethphage, located on the eastern slope of the Mount of Olives near Jerusalem. There Jesus told two of his disciples, "Go your way into the village over against you: and as soon as ye be entered into it, ye shall find a colt tied, whereon never man sat; loose him, and bring him. And if any man say unto you, Why do ye this? say ye that the Lord hath need of him; and straightway he will send him hither" (Mark 11:2-3).

His request, which did not include compensation for use of the animal, seems unusual to a Westerner. However, it was an appropriate request during the festive season of Passover, when hospitality was generously offered to friends and strangers alike. Devout Jews hung curtains in front of their doors as a sign that all passersby were welcome. They offered bed and board to strangers, and loaned animals upon request. "Take it, kill it if you

◄ Bas relief sculpture in the Garden of Gethsemane.

◄ (opposite page) Olive trees in the traditional site of the Garden of Gethsemane on the Mount of Olives. Some of these trees are as old as 2,000 years.

❧ ▲ The leaves of a fig tree.

❧ ▶ A date palm plantation located at En Gedi, near the Dead Sea.

❧ ▶ (opposite page) A donkey is tied to an archway outside the Old City of Jerusalem.

wish, it is yours," the owner of an animal often replied to a request.[1]

With the colt in their possession, the disciples returned to Bethpage and gave the animal to Jesus. They then spread their garments on the back of the colt, and the Master sat atop—an ancient gesture signaling royalty to the Jews and fulfilling the prophecy, "thy King cometh unto thee, meek, and sitting upon an ass" (Matthew 21:5). Riding the colt, Jesus ascended from Bethpage to the Kidron Valley, and then rode up to the Holy City.

His entrance into the city was nothing short of the triumphant entry of a king. Roman soldiers did not stop the pomp and circumstances of his entrance or think him a revolutionary, an aspiring king, or a fanatic planning religious anarchy. Although soldiers in the name of the Roman Empire had suppressed Druids for practicing human sacrifice, Phoenicians for casting children into sacrificial fire, and fanatics with Messianic claims, a humble Jew on a donkey laden with common garments entering Jerusalem did not pose a threat. If Jesus had ridden a horse into the Holy City, his actions would have symbolized war against Rome and perhaps triggered bloodshed. But Jesus was not a warring conqueror. He was the Messiah, the Son of God, the Prince of Peace.

As a "very great multitude" of Jewish pilgrims saw him enter Jerusalem on a donkey laden with garments, they "spread their garments in the way; others cut down branches from the trees, and strawed them in the way" (Matthew 21:8). They then waved the branches, a symbol of Jewish patriotism since the Hasmonaean period.[2] "Hosanna to the Son of David," shouted the multitude (Matthew 21:9). "Blessed is he that cometh in the name of the Lord; Hosanna in the highest" (Matthew 21:9).[3]

After his triumphal entry, Jesus, like other pilgrims to the Holy City, went up to the Temple Mount. (See Mark

Whitewashed graves are seen on the Mount of Olives. Jesus compared Pharisees to "whited sepulchres" (Matthew 23:27).

Modern-day Bethany has ancient and new structures side-by-side.

Near the Temple Mount are fonts used by Muslims to ceremoniously wash themselves.

(opposite page) The Gate Beautiful or Golden Gate is on the east side of Jerusalem and faces the Mount of Olives, where many graves are located. Jews believe that the Messiah will enter Jerusalem through this gate.

11:11.) Within the shadows of the Temple, he wept as he thought of the future destruction of the house of the Lord and the Holy City. When eventide came, he left the Holy City and rested in Bethany with his chosen twelve.

The next day, he returned to Jerusalem and once again entered the Temple Mount. There he "cast out" those trafficking in sacrificial offerings and those who bought the tainted merchandise (Luke 19:45). "My house is the house of prayer," he exclaimed. "Ye have made it a den of thieves" (Luke 19:46). Although his words and actions were offensive to the merchants and moneychangers, it was the chief priests and scribes who sought to destroy him. These leaders were prevented from their wicked course that day, for

"all the people were very attentive to hear [Jesus]" (Luke 19:48). And again, "when even was come, he went out of the city" (Mark 11:19).

On the third day, Jesus went up again to the temple courts. On the Mount, Jewish leaders questioned his authority. In answer to their queries, Jesus told the parables of the two sons (Matthew 21:28-31), the wicked husbandmen (Matthew 21:33-44), and the marriage of the king's son (Matthew 22:2-14).[4] The leaders were angry with Jesus, "for they knew that he had spoken the parable[s] against them" (Mark 12:12). They sought to "lay hold on him, but [they] feared the people" (Mark 12:12).

Feeling their power weakened by the mere presence of Jesus in the temple courts, the Pharisees took counsel from their political enemies, the Herodians.[5] The Herodians and Pharisees were willing to lay aside years of verbal disputes and partisan politics to find fault with Jesus and put him to death. With evil intent in their hearts, the Herodians asked Jesus, "What thinkest thou? Is it lawful to give tribute unto Caesar, or not?" (Matthew 22:17). Jesus perceived their wicked design and said to the conspirators, "Why tempt ye me, ye hypocrites?" (Matthew 22:18). When the prideful Sadducees questioned him further, he said, "Ye do err, not knowing the scriptures, nor the power of God" (Matthew 22:29).[6]

His answers upset the Jewish factions present on the Temple Mount that day. His statement, "Woe unto you, scribes and Pharisee, hypocrites: . . . ye outwardly appear righteous unto men, but within ye are full of hypocrisy and iniquity . . . Ye serpents, ye generation of vipers, how can ye escape the damnation of hell?" was most offensive to the Jewish leaders (Matthew 23:14, 28, 33).[7] Yet they were powerless before Jesus. The multitude listened to the man who had entered Jerusalem as a Jewish king and now cried,

"O Jerusalem, Jerusalem, thou that killest the prophets, and stonest them which are sent unto thee, how often would I have gathered thy children together, even as a hen gathereth her chickens under her wings, and ye would not! Behold, your house is left unto you desolate" (Matthew 23:37-38).

Later in the day, Jesus left the Temple Mount with his disciples and climbed the Mount of Olives. (See Matthew 24:1.) There he foretold future events, including the destruction of the temple. "There shall not be left here one stone upon another, that shall not be thrown down," Jesus prophesied (Matthew 24:2). His disciples wondered at his sayings and asked when the temple would be destroyed, the Jews scattered, and the Son of Man come in glory.

Through parables and vivid descriptions, Jesus spoke indirectly of many events that would transpire before all things would be fulfilled and the Son of Man come in glory. But directly he said, "Of that day and hour knoweth no man, no, not the angels of heaven, but my Father only" (Matthew 24:36). He then assured his disciples that when the Lord came in his glory, with all his holy angels, the righteous would receive eternal life.

In the evening, Jesus went to the village of Bethany and the house of Simon the leper.[8] As he sat with Simon and his friend Lazarus, he was served supper by Martha, the sister of Lazarus. During the meal another sister, Mary, poured costly spikenard ointment from an alabaster box on the feet of Jesus. Her anointing displayed singular regard, a "reverential homage rarely rendered even to kings" on their coronation day.[9]

Of those who witnessed Mary's generous act, only Judas was angry. His anger did not stem from love of the poor, but from personal greed. "To what purpose is this waste?" he asked, knowing that the ointment "might have been sold

▲ Phylacteries, meaning amulets or small boxes fastened with leather cords to the forehead or arm, contain small strips of parchment inscribed with sacred text.

▶ Issa, an Arab hacker, holds ancient Jewish and Roman coins in his hands.

▶ (opposite page) Mark 12:41-44 recounts the poor widow's contribution to the temple treasury.

▶ (opposite page) Branch of an olive tree in bloom.

for much" (Matthew 26:8-9). Jesus replied, "Why trouble ye the woman? for she hath wrought a good work upon me" (Matthew 26:10). But Judas was troubled. He left Simon's house and went directly to the chief priests in Jerusalem—those who could incite the masses against Jesus and lead multitudes to reject their king. The priests encouraged the betrayal of Judas and offered to reward him for his sin.

"What will ye give me, and I will deliver [Jesus] unto you?" Judas asked (Matthew 26:15). With the temple treasury at their disposal, the chief priests could have given a thousand silver pieces or more. However, a token price of thirty pieces of silver was agreed upon—one-tenth or perhaps a tithe of the cost of the ointment Mary had poured on the feet of Jesus.[10] Would Judas rob God for a tithe? Yes! For he, like the merchants and money changers on the Temple Mount, was a thief in the House of Judah. The luciferic covenant struck between the priests and Judas is the last recorded event of the third day of the Passover festivities.

There is no record of the activity or teachings of Jesus on the fourth day of that holy week. It is assumed that he did not go to the Temple Mount, where thousands of Paschal lambs were slaughtered by representatives of families or companies for the Paschal Supper. If this assumption is correct, he would not have seen the estimated 260,000 lambs slaughtered or their remains carried by men as they descended from the Temple Mount to nearby homes.

On the fifth day, Jesus went again into Jerusalem and there partook of the Passover Feast, a symbolic dinner held in remembrance of the angel of death passing over the homes and flocks of Israel before the exodus from Egypt.

In preparation for the feast, Jesus instructed Peter and John to "Go into the city," meaning the Holy City, and "there shall a man meet you, bearing a pitcher of water" drawn from the pool of Siloam; "follow him" (Matthew

26;18; Luke 22:10). He directed them to say to the man, "The Master saith unto thee, Where is the guest chamber, where I shall eat the passover with my disciples? And he shall shew you a large upper room furnished: there make ready" (Luke 22:11-12).

Peter and John did as Jesus asked, and went to the pool of Siloam. There they saw a man with a pitcher of water, and followed him to his home. After saying to the man, "The Master saith unto thee, Where is the guest chamber, where I shall eat the passover with my disciples?," Peter and John were shown a large upper chamber or guest-chamber located on the roof of his home (Luke 22:11). Reached by climbing outside stairs, it was a choice setting for the Passover Feast.

The chamber was proffered and then prepared for the festive occasion by Peter, John, and the good man of the house. Rugs, pillows, divans, and tables were made ready.[11] Lamb was roasted on a pomegranate spit, lamps were lit, unleavened cakes baked, and bitter herbs gathered. When the preparations were finished, Peter and John left the home of the good man, seeking Jesus.

After finding him, they led the Lord and the other apostles to the upper chamber to eat the Passover Feast. After entering the chamber, Jesus "sat down with the twelve" (Matthew 26:20). Some of them, like the Pharisees and Sadducees clamoring for the chief seats in the synagogues, quarreled over who would recline next to Jesus. They knew that it was customary for the host of the feast, in this case Jesus, to have his choicest friends seated on his left and on his right side.

We assume Judas was given the place of honor, which was on the left side of Jesus. John the Beloved received the second place of honor, and was seated on his right.[12] Jesus then said, "With desire I have desired to eat this passover with you before I suffer: For I say unto you, I will not any more eat thereof, until it be fulfilled in the kingdom of God" (Luke 22:15-16). The meal then began.

Formal Passover procedures have varied through the centuries, so it is difficult to say with certainty the exact steps of the meal that Jesus and the twelve followed. However, it is known that during the course of the meal, Jesus "riseth from supper, and laid aside his garments; and took a towel, and girded himself. After that he poureth water into a basin, and began to wash the disciples' feet" (John 13:4-5). His actions, mirroring those of a common slave, were unsettling to Peter. "Thou shalt never wash my feet," he exclaimed (John 13:8). Jesus said, "If I wash thee not, thou hast no part with me" (John 13:8). Peter responded, "Lord, not my feet only, but also my hands and my head" (John 13:9). Jesus then pronounced his apostles "clean every whit . . . but not all" (John 13:10).

The "not all" was explained after Jesus removed the towel from his waist and lay down to eat. As the dining commenced, Jesus said, "Verily I say unto you, that one of you shall betray me . . . woe unto that man by whom the Son of man is betrayed! it had been good for that man if he had not been born" (Matthew 26:21, 24). Those seated at the feast were sorrowful at his declaration and began to ask, "Lord, is it I?" (Matthew 26:22). Jesus answered, "He it is, to whom I shall give a sop, when I have dipped it" (John 13:26). Judas asked, "Is it I?" (Matthew 26:25). Jesus replied, "Thou hast said . . . And when he had dipped the sop, he gave it to Judas" (Matthew 26:25; John 13:26).

Judas accepted the sop, yet did not finish the meal, for "Satan entered into him" (John 13:27). Jesus then said to Judas, "That thou doest, do quickly" (John 13:27). It is probable that the other apostles were unaware of Judas' betrayal, and supposed that as the treasurer of the twelve, he was leaving the feast to purchase a gift for the poor—a Passover custom.

After Judas left the upper room, and while those who remained were still eating, Jesus took the round, unleavened bread and "blessed it, and brake it, and gave it to the disciples, and said, Take, eat; this is my body" or as Luke reports, "This do in remembrance of me" (Matthew 26:26; Luke 22:19). He next "took the cup, and gave thanks, and gave it to them, saying, Drink ye all of it; For this is my blood of the new testament, which is shed for many for the remission of sins" (Matthew 26:27-28).

Jesus then said to his faithful apostles, "Peace I leave with you, my peace I give unto you: not as the world giveth, give I unto you. Let not your heart be troubled, neither let it be afraid" (John 14:27). With this gift of peace, Jesus gave them a new commandment—"That ye love one another; as I have loved you, that ye also love one another. By this shall all men know that ye are my disciples, if ye have love one to another" (John 13:34-35).

This alabaster jar is carved from a solid piece of stone. Inside such jars, precious ointments and spices were stored during the days of Jesus.

(opposite page) Bags of spices in the market at Nazareth.

Jesus showed his love for the apostles in the Intercessory or High Priestly Prayer. In the prayer he offered himself as a ransom for the sins of the world, announced the completion of his mortal ministry, and pleaded in behalf of his faithful apostles and those who would believe their teachings. Then it was time for him to show even greater love—but the upper room was not the right setting.

Jesus and his faithful disciples left the upper room and the Holy City of Jerusalem. They crossed the Kidron Valley and climbed up the slope of Mount Olivet[13] to an olive orchard known as Gethsemane.[14] Then Jesus said, "All ye shall be offended because of me this night: for it is written, I will smite the shepherd, and the sheep of the flock shall be scattered abroad" (Matthew 16:31). Peter attempted to assure the Lord that he would not be offended, but the Master knew better. "Before the cock crow, thou shalt deny me thrice," he said to Peter (Matthew 26:34). He then told his disciples, "Sit ye here, while I go and pray yonder" (Matthew 26:36).

He took only Peter, James, and John with him into a secluded area of the garden of Gethsemane. When he "began to be sorrowful and very heavy," he said to these three, "My soul is exceeding sorrowful, even unto death: tarry ye here, and watch with me" (Matthew 26:38).[15] Jesus went alone "about a stone's cast," or a hundred feet away, and knelt in supplication to God (Luke 22:41). "O my Father," he prayed, "if it be possible, let this cup pass from me: nevertheless not as I will, but as thou wilt" (Matthew 26:39).

"This was Jesus' appointed hour—the hour for which he came into the world; the hour when he would take upon himself the sins of the world. For this purpose was he born; for this purpose had he lived. . . . There is no mystery to compare with the mystery of redemption . . . Finite minds

can no more comprehend how and in what manner Jesus performed his redeeming labors than they can comprehend how matter came into being, or how Gods began to be. . . . We may not intrude too closely into this scene. It is shrouded in a halo and a mystery into which no footstep may penetrate."[16]

Yet, we know that in Gethsemane he "descended below all things as he prepared himself to rise above them all." Jesus "suffered the pain of all men, that all men might repent and come unto him."[17] For as Isaiah prophesied, "All we like sheep have gone astray; we have turned every one to his own way; and the Lord hath laid on him the iniquity of us all. . . . Surely he hath borne our griefs, and carried our sorrows" (Isaiah 53:4, 6).

⁂ ▲ *The triclinium table is set for a traditional Passover Feast at the Biblical Resources Pilgrim Center in Jerusalem.*

⁂ ◄ *The hall of the Last Supper in the Dormition Abbey is located in the upper part of Jerusalem.*

⁂ ◄ *(opposite page) Rock basins were anciently used for washing feet.*

73

CHAPTER 8

BETRAYAL TO JUDGMENT

This stone tablet dates to the first century. It confirms that Pontius Pilate was the Prefect of Judaea.

(opposite page) One of many thorn bushes growing in the Holy Land.

PHOTOGRAPHER'S NOTE - MAY 10-11, 1998
FULL MOON OVER JERUSALEM

Could it be that on the most important days in the history of Christianity, Judaism, and Jerusalem, there has been a full moon in the sky? Passover occurs on the first full moon following the first day of spring, and even the Jewish calendar is based on the phases of the moon. I think there is great significance to the full moon over Jerusalem.

While many photographers have captured beautiful images of Jerusalem with sunsets, I wanted my photograph to have a full moon. But how? When would the full moon appear? I prayed to God that the weather would cooperate and that I might photograph a full moon.

The days leading up to May 10th were hot, with much haze and dust in the air. I hadn't seen a moon rise or set. I talked to Steven Rona about taking me to the Mount of Olives on both the morning of the 9th and 10th of May to see what would happen in the sky.

At 4:30 a.m. on May 9th, we drove to the Mount of Olives. Wind was blowing, and the haze and fog were so heavy that we could barely see the city, let alone a moon. I made a couple of exposures anyway, just because we were there. The next morning, we awoke at 4:00 a.m. and went outside to look. Fog had settled over Jerusalem.

"Fog!" I thought. "In Jerusalem!" I went back to bed discouraged, thinking I had lost my last chance to photograph a full moon over Jerusalem.

It continued foggy most of the day, but in the afternoon it started to clear. By 4:00 p.m. the sun was shining. I asked Ofer, an employee of Israel Revealed, where I could photograph the sunset from the west side of the city, looking east. He suggested the top of the YMCA tower. "Can you get me up there?" I asked.

"I'll check," he replied.

"Will you go with me?" I asked, knowing it was after hours for him. "Sure," he said with a slight hint of reluctance. He called me at 5:00 p.m. and said, "We have two tickets to get into the tower. Meet me at 6:30."

Daniel and Marilyn Rona drove with me to the tower. "Too bad about the moon," Daniel said.

"I guess it wasn't to be," was my disappointed reply.

At the YMCA tower I met Ofer. We took the elevator to the observation deck, a very small balcony on the fourteenth floor, only to find that we had a great view of the King David Hotel, but not the Old City. Seeing the King Solomon Hotel a couple of blocks south of the tower, Ofer suggested that we go there to photograph.

At the hotel, Ofer spoke in Hebrew to the clerk at the front desk, who, in turn, paged the security guard, who then called the manager. They checked to see if a room on the fifteenth floor was vacant and finally said, "Okay, but only for fifteen minutes."

"If we have only fifteen minutes, let's wait until 7:15 p.m. to go up. That will give us the best sunset time," I said. We waited and then went up. The last rays of sunlight were glowing on the city walls when we stepped onto the large balcony of a penthouse. I quickly set up the 4X5 camera, calculated exposures and began exposing film, first with the 6X12 cm panorama back and then with full 4X5 inch sheets.

Ofer and the security guard talked in Hebrew as I worked. At the end of fifteen minutes, I began putting things away. "This is the best view of Jerusalem anywhere in the city," the security guard said in nearly perfect English, which startled me. "It's really good when the lights of the city come on. I've got some good pictures from here," he continued, revealing that he wants to become a photographer himself. He asked a few questions about my equipment and then said, "You ought to come back some night, later."

"I was hoping to stay for an hour tonight," I replied. "But all they would give us was fifteen minutes."

"Well, the manager hasn't called me to have you leave. Maybe my radio is broken," he said with a wink.

I put the lens back on the camera. The lights of the city were starting to glow, and just above the eastern horizon, through a light haze, a full orange moon was rising. My prayer had been answered. I photographed for another thirty minutes as the full moon rose into a clear sky over Jerusalem.

While Jesus was speaking with his apostles in Gethsemane, "Judas, one of the twelve" unashamedly approached the hallowed garden (Matthew 26:47).[1] With him were a multitude of boisterous men armed with staves and swords. These men were confident that the traitor would lead them to Jesus of Nazareth, and upon finding him, an agreed-upon sign would be given:

(opposite page) Tradition suggests that Jesus climbed these 2,000-year-old steps when led to the palace of Caiaphas.

Potter's Field, often referred to as the Field of Blood, is where Judas hanged himself.

"Whomsoever [Judas] shall kiss, that same is he: hold him fast" (Matthew 26:48).

Judas chose a traitor's kiss to single out the Son of God from the Galilean apostles gathered that night in Gethsemane—a mockery of the compassion of Jesus' ministry. Adding to the oddity of the traitor's feigned love of the Master is the Greek translation of the betrayer's kiss, which implies that Judas "not only kissed but covered Him with kisses, kissed Him repeatedly, loudly, effusively."[2]

When the sign was given, those in the multitude with staves and swords stepped forward and "laid hands on Jesus, and took him" (Matthew 26:50). The impetuous Peter drew his sword, a gladius with a blade about twenty inches long, from under his upper garment and struck Malchus, "a servant of the high priest's, and smote off his ear" (Matthew 26:51). "Put up again thy sword into his place," Jesus said to Peter, "for all they that take the sword shall perish with the sword" (Matthew 26:52). By a mere touch of the Master's hand, the damage Peter had caused to the ear of Malchus was healed. (See Luke 22:51.)

"Thinkest thou that I cannot now pray to my Father, and he shall presently give me more than twelve legions of angels?" Jesus asked. "But how then shall the scriptures be fulfilled?" (Matthew 26:53-54). To fulfill all righteousness, Jesus consented to the illegal arrest at Gethsemane and permitted himself to be bound and taken prisoner. His atoning hours in prayer were now finished, and the workers of evil would have their way.

Jesus was taken by the "captain and officers of the Jews" from Gethsemane to the home or palace of Annas, the "most influential Jew of his day" (John 18:12).[3] From there he was taken to the palace of Joseph Caiaphas, the High Priest. Awaiting his arrival in the palace was an assembly of twenty-three leading elders, scribes, and chief priests, all

❧ ▲ *Stone pavement in the judg-ment hall in the Antonia fortress where Jesus was scourged and spat upon by Roman soldiers.*

❧ ▶ *On the pavement stones are signs of games played by the Roman soldiers.*

members of the Great Sanhedrin. They formed a quorum or council of the highest Jewish tribunal as they sat waiting to judge the Son of God.[4] They had the power to judge both civil and criminal charges, and could pass and impose judgment for wrongdoing. Yet under Roman rule, the Sanhedrin had no authority to execute a judgment of death by crucifixion—an imposing obstacle to their evil designs that evening.

Another limiting factor was the regulation governing trial procedures for a capital offense. If the prisoner was found guilty of the offense, a second trial was required. In preparation for the second trial, members of the Sanhedrin were asked to fast and pray before the trial commenced. At the second trial, those who had voted against the prisoner in the first trial could reverse their judgment, but those who voted for an acquittal were bound by their vote. If all members of the Sanhedrin voted to convict the prisoner of a capital charge, the verdict was void because the accused had no defender.

With these restrictions clearly in mind, let us review the trial of Jesus in the palace of Caiaphas. We know that he was mocked, smitten, and blindfolded. Although such actions were reprehensible, the greatest offense came from the High Priest, Caiaphas, who presided over the Sanhedrin and administered the religious and internal affairs of the Jews. He asked Jesus, "Art thou the Christ, the Son of the Blessed?" (Mark 14:61). Without equivocation the Savior responded, "I am: and ye shall see the Son of man sitting on the right hand of power, and coming in the clouds of heaven" (Mark 14:62).

His unabashed, truthful response raised the issue of blasphemy. The words "blessed" and "power" were understood by Jewish leaders to mean God. According to the assembled members of the Sanhedrin, Jesus was "claiming for human or demon power the prerogatives of God, or in dishonoring God by ascribing to Him[self] attributes short of perfection."[5] By his words, the High Priest concluded that Jesus had committed an enormous crime—the crime of blasphemy. Caiaphas, in a theatrical display of grief and horror, stood up and rent his outer and inner garments about eight inches. Jewish law prescribed that members of the Sanhedrin, in sympathy with the High Priest, should arise and likewise rend their garments.

"What need we any further witnesses?" asked Caiaphas. "Ye have heard the blasphemy: what think ye?" (Mark 14:63-64). "He is guilty of death," exclaimed the Sanhedrin (Matthew 26:66). To them, the Son of God was unclean and defiled. The council then arose and came forward and spat on the face of Jesus, which in Judaism signified their refusal to share his guilt. (See Matthew 26:67.) They then "buffeted him; and others smote him with the palms of their hands," and said to the blindfolded Savior, "Prophesy unto us thou Christ, Who is he that smote thee?" (Matthew 26:68). Following this trial, there was a delay before the second trial commenced in the early dawn hours. During the delay, temple guards, captains, and many observers—the curious, the malcontent, and at least one faithful disciple, Peter— waited outside the palace for further news of the judicial proceedings. For those who waited, "a fire of coals [was made]; for it was cold: and they warmed themselves" (John 18:18). As the observers gathered around the fire, a damsel asked Peter, "Art not thou also one of this man's disciples?" (John 18:17). Peter answered, "I am not" (John 18:17). Again he was asked the same question, and again he answered, "I am not" (John 18:25). As Peter persisted in his denial, a servant asked, "Did not I see thee in the garden with him?" (John 18:26). Again the denial came, but this time it was followed by the crowing of the cock.[6]

The "crowing" was probably bugle notes played by a soldier from atop the Antonia fortress. The notes signaled a change in the Roman guard and closed the third watch, which the Romans called "cockcrow." Sometime after cock-

▲ The garment Jesus wore, over which the soldiers cast lots, could have been a talith or prayer shawl similar to the one depicted here.

crow, the second trial began. Members of the Sanhedrin who had participated in the first trial had less than three hours to prepare for the second. About six in the morning, under a veiled pretense of legality, a full quorum of the Sanhedrin met and "took counsel against Jesus to put him to death" (Matthew 27:1).

Details of the trial are lacking, but in the end, Jesus was judged guilty of blasphemy, and according to rabbinic law must die by stoning and then have his body suspended from a tree.

The verdict had been rendered, but there arose the question of how to execute the judgment. "When the morning was come, all the chief priests and elders of the people took counsel" as to how to put Jesus to death (Matthew 27:1). The decision reached was to lead Jesus "away, and [deliver] him to Pontius Pilate the governor," who had power to inflict the death penalty of crucifixion (Matthew 27:2). Pilate was temporarily residing in the Antonia fortress in Jerusalem. He had not left the splendor of Caesarea to be in Jerusalem as a worshipful pilgrim, but was in the Holy City to maintain order during the festivities.

Caiaphas, members of the Sanhedrin, temple guards, and probably Annas led the prisoner to the Antonia fortress.[7] Near the fortress, temple guards turned Jesus over to the Roman soldiers. They, like the Jewish leaders, would not enter the fortress, believing that if they did enter, they would be defiled because a Gentile was within. Yet they had no qualms about giving Jesus over to a Gentile. From outside the walls, they loudly accused Jesus of sedition and treason.

In these morning hours, as Jewish leaders cried against Jesus, there was one in Jerusalem who was remorseful. Judas, having learned the verdict of the Sanhedrin, attempted to repent by returning the pieces of silver to the chief priests and elders. "I have sinned in that I have betrayed the innocent blood," he said as he proffered the silver (Matthew 27:4). The Jewish leaders mocked his repentance. "What is that to us?" they scoffed (Matthew 27:4). Judas "cast down the pieces of silver in the temple" and went outside the city gates to a clay yard.[8] There, fully aware of his sin, he hanged himself on a tree.

At or near the time of Judas' hanging, an innocent Jesus "stood before the governor" Pontius Pilate in the hall of judgment in the Antonia fortress (Matthew 27:11). "Art thou the King of the Jews?" asked Pilate of Jesus (Matthew 27:11). Jesus replied, "Thou sayest" (Matthew 27:11). Pilate, hearing the accusations of the chief priest and elders from outside the walls, asked Jesus, "Hearest thou not how many things they witness against thee?" (Matthew 27:13). But Jesus "answered him to never a word; insomuch that the governor marvelled greatly" (Matthew 27:14).

Perhaps in frustration, Pilate went out to the Jewish leaders and asked, "What accusation bring ye against this man?" (John 18:29). "If he were not a malefactor, we would not have delivered him up unto thee," they replied (John 18:30). Then Pilate said, "Take ye him, and judge him

according to your law" (John 18:31). The Jewish leaders did not reveal to the Roman ruler that they had already judged him, but instead declared, "It is not lawful for us to put any man to death" (John 18:31).

After listening to their rationale, Pilate entered the judgment hall again. He asked Jesus, "Art thou King of the Jews?" (John 18:33). Jesus answered, "Sayest thou this thing of thyself, or did others tell it thee of me?" (John 18:34). Pilate answered, "Am I a Jew? Thine own nation and the chief priests have delivered thee unto me: what hast thou done?" (John 18:35). Jesus answered, "My kingdom is not of this world: if my kingdom were of this world, then would my servants fight, that I should not be delivered to the Jews" (John 18:36).

(opposite page, both photos) Beneath the replica of the Palace of Caiaphas are dungeon-like rooms. Atop the structure is a rooster weather vane, symbolic of the Savior's prophecy that Peter would deny him three times before the cock crowed.

Herod's palace as depicted in the Model City.

Caesarea was built by King Herod on the sandy Mediterranean coast. This "Rome" away from Rome had a sports arena, splendid theater, a breakwater harbor, and an aqueduct that brought fresh water thirteen miles from Mt. Carmel to the city.

After further deliberation, Pilate went again among the Jews outside the walls of the fortress and said to them, "I find in [Jesus] no fault at all" (John 18:38). Jewish leaders were angry at the apparent Roman acquittal and hurled additional charges against Jesus, still hoping for a verdict that would lead to his death. From the Gospel of Mark we learn that "the chief priests accused him of many things," but Jesus "answered nothing" (Mark 15:3).

Frustrated with his Jewish subjects and perhaps looking for an escape from this mounting dilemma, Pilate, knowing that Jesus was a Galilean, proposed that the prisoner be sent to Herod Antipas, the Roman appointed tetrarch over Galilee. Herod was in Jerusalem for the Passover festivities and was probably residing in the old Hasmonean palace, which had been the royal residence of the Herods before the Antonia fortress was constructed. (See Luke 23:6-7.) Herod was pleased that Pilate would send Jesus to him. He had wanted to talk to this Galilean since the death of John the Baptist, and was "exceeding glad" to see him (Luke 23:8).

As he interrogated the Son of God, Herod demanded to be shown a great miracle. Jesus did not respond to his demands. Even when "the chief priest and scribes stood and vehemently accused him," Jesus was silent. His silence was foretold by Isaiah: "He was oppressed, and he was afflicted, yet he opened not his mouth" (Isaiah 53:7).

Before returning the condemned Jesus to Pilate, "Herod with his men of war set him at nought, and mocked him, and arrayed him in a gorgeous robe" (Luke 23:11). We assume that the robe draped across his shoulders was a white outer garment, the apparel worn by Jewish nobility and the festive clothing worn by pilgrims during the Passover week. Once adorned, Jesus was returned to Pilate.

With the burden of judgment again resting on the Gentile governor, the case against Jesus still hung in the balance. Hoping to tip the scales of justice in favor of the Galilean, "for [Pilate] knew that for envy they had delivered him," the governor proposed to release a Jewish prisoner as was the Roman custom during the Passover festivities (Matthew 27:18). "Whom will ye that I release unto you?" he asked the people—"Barabbas, or Jesus which is called Christ?" (Matthew 27:17). Although his wife warned him, "Have thou nothing to do with that just man: for I have suffered many things this day in a dream because of him," his words had been said, and the crowd outside the fortress was ready to choose (Matthew 27:19).[9]

Barabbas was their choice. Although he had incited an insurrection and committed murder, he was the man the crowd chose. "What shall I do then with Jesus which is called Christ?" asked Pilate (Matthew 27:22). The unequivocal answer was, "Let him be crucified" (Matthew 27:22). Their choice of crucifixion was the most cruel and hideous of punishments inflicted on a prisoner in the Roman empire. Since this punishment was only to be executed on rebels against Rome, delinquent slaves, robbers and deserters, and those who committed a barbarous offense, Pilate questioned the choice of the Jews. Having found Jesus innocent, he asked, "Why, what evil hath he done?" (Matthew 27:23). But the agitated crowd yelled all the more vehemently, "Let him be crucified" (Matthew

27:23), which in Jewish terminology meant "Let the commended be cursed."[10]

When Pilate failed to sway the opinion of the chief priests, elders, and the multitude outside the fortress, he performed two symbolic acts as a witness that he found Jesus innocent. One was a Gentile witness and the other a Jewish witness. The Gentile witness occurred when he arose from the judgment seat before issuing his decree, which was a Gentile symbol of innocence. The Jewish witness was to wash "his hands before the multitude" (Matthew 27:24). By this action, he showed the Jews that he disclaimed responsibility for the sentence of death that would be pronounced. "I am innocent of the blood of this just person: see ye to it," Pilate said after washing his hands (Matthew 27:24). The crowd yelled, "His blood be on us, and on our children" (Matthew 27:25). Barabbas was then released, and Jesus was forcefully taken away from the judgment hall to a common hall, where "the whole band of soldiers" had gathered waiting for the condemned (Matthew 27:27).

Aloe vera plants near the entrance of the Roman Theatre in Caesarea.

Roman Theatre and ancient ruins in Caesarea.

It was a custom among the Syrian soldiers employed by Rome to mock the condemned before execution of the penalty. Since Jesus had gained significant recognition during his multiple trials before the leaders of Judaism and Rome, the mockery was intense. With Pilate watching, the soldiers stripped off Jesus' garments and strapped him to a pillar or frame. Then they beat him or scourged him with a whip. The three leather thongs on the whip were weighted with sharp pieces of stone, lead balls, and sheep bone.

Jesus was then unstrapped from the pillar and attired in a makeshift kingly fashion. A short scarlet or purple sagum, a woolen war cloak often worn by Roman generals, was fastened by a clasp over his right shoulder.[11] A twisted garland of thorns was placed upon his head, and a reed put in his right hand. The soldiers then bowed their knees as they approached Jesus, saying, "Hail, King of the Jews!" (Matthew 27:29). They then spat on him, took the reed, and struck him on the head.

After the mockery and beating, Jesus was presented to the crowd still waiting outside the Antonia fortress. Pilate asked the Jewish leaders and the multitude standing near the fortress to spare the life of Jesus, but they would not. "Behold your King!" Pilate said (John 19:14). But the ruling Jews cried out, "Away with him, away with him, crucify him" (John 19:15). "Shall I crucify your King?" Pilate asked (John 19:15). The chief priests replied, "We have no king but Caesar" (John 19:15).[12]

ॐ . . . . *I am the light of the world;*
he that followeth me shall not walk in
darkness, but shall have the light of life.
(John 8:12)

CHAPTER 9

FROM GOLGOTHA TO THE GARDEN

PHOTOGRAPHER'S NOTE - MAY 18, 1998
LAST DAY

This is my last day in Jerusalem. The last day to visit Bethany, the Mount of Olives, Gethsemane, Caiaphas' palace, the Antonia fortress, Golgotha, and the Garden Tomb.

With the sun hanging low in the western sky and strains of "I Know That My Redeemer Lives" ringing in my ears, I sit in quiet solitude near the Garden Tomb from where Christ arose, glorified and resurrected. All is peaceful, and I savor the sight. My trip is over. The last picture has been taken, the last roll of film exposed. I sit quietly in the late afternoon, bathing in the spirit of the garden.

Entering the tomb in peaceful solitude, I can see in my mind the Savior's body lying in the borrowed sepulchre, wrapped in burial clothes. His head is nearest to where I stand and his feet stretched out away from me toward the opposite wall. I can envision three days later, when those same burial clothes were neatly folded and two angels stood at opposite ends of the burial

chamber, announcing, "He is not here: for he is risen" (Matthew 28:6).

Returning to my place outside the tomb, I can see the glorious morning when Mary found the tomb empty, and heard the Resurrected Lord speak her name. She was the first of many to see the glorified Savior. In the peaceful garden, I sense the beauty of that morning—full of light.

My serenity and solitude are interrupted as a tour group passes in front of me, wanting to see the tomb where Jesus had lain. My initial reaction is disappointment as the peace of the moment is broken. But as they file into the tomb, speaking an unfamiliar tongue, I see that they, too, are seeking Jesus. "He rose for them, also," I muse. His resurrection is not just for me. His resurrection is universal—for everyone.

A cool breeze sifts through the garden, carrying with it the sweet fragrances of hundreds of colorful flowers. The chaos of the Old City, though only a few blocks away, seems far distant. I strain to capture every nuance of the scene, memorizing each detail, scent, and feeling, knowing that tomorrow when I see the

(opposite page) "Now in the place where he was crucified there was a garden; and in the garden a new sepulchre, wherein was never a man yet laid" (John 19:41). The Garden Tomb is located less than a hundred paces from Golgotha.

The fragrance and beauty of thousands of flowers like these calla lilies fill the peaceful garden near the Garden Tomb.

▲ *Of the eight gates in the Old City of Jerusalem, the Damascus Gate is the most ornate and beautiful.*

streets of Jerusalem along a route later designated *Via Dolorosa*. During this particular procession, in which Jesus of Nazareth was the focal point, Jewish women cried aloud in commiseration and praise of the condemned as he passed by. (See Luke 23:27.) A few of the women, like generations of women before them, prepared an aromatic potion called gall, which would later be offered to the condemned Savior and the two thieves to ease their pain.

According to Christian tradition, Jesus carried the patibulum or crossbar from the hall of judgment to the city gate of Jerusalem before soldiers compelled "Simon a Cyrenian, . . . to bear his cross" (Mark 15:21).[2]

The procession halted about a third of a mile from the city gate at "Golgotha, which is, being interpreted, The place of a skull" (Mark 15:22).[3] There Jesus was offered "vinegar to drink mingled with gall," a mixture intended to deaden his sensibility and ease the pain of his crucifixion (Matthew 27:33-34).[4] He refused the mixture. Therefore, Jesus was fully aware of the cruelty inflicted by the soldiers as they nailed him to the crossbar. Iron nails were hammered into the palms of his hands and between the bones of each wrist, "probably piercing the median nerve in the wrists and causing intense pain."[5]

He then was lifted up and attached to the endbar as nails were hammered into his feet. To prevent the weight of his body from pulling away from the endbar, we assume a prop was placed between his legs and beneath his feet, forming a narrow seat. Early Christian artists depicted the prop as if Jesus were "sitting on a throne" while hanging on the cross.[6] Above his head was nailed a titulus penned by Pontius Pilate: "Jesus of Nazareth the King of the Jews" (John 19:19).[7]

Whether the crossbar attached to the endbar formed a cross shaped like an "X" (Crux Decussata), a "T" (Crux

setting sun, I will be home, and this will be but a memory—a memory I will hold forever.

Without delay, Pilate turned the prisoner over to his soldiers to execute the judgment of crucifixion.[1] Jesus was taken from the hall of judgment and led outside the Antonia fortress. Once outside of the garrison, a military procession was formed. During the procession the condemned—Jesus and two convicted thieves, each carrying a heavy wooden crossbar—were guarded by soldiers. Military processions moving toward Golgotha attracted large numbers of pilgrims as they marched through the

Commissa), or a "t" (Crux Immissa) is not known. All three types of crosses were used in provinces throughout the Roman empire at the time of Jesus. However, it is known that the condemned hung low on the cross so that physical and verbal abuse was still possible.

Interspersed between the volleys of abuse Jesus suffered as he hung from the cross are remembered, even choice sayings. "Father, forgive them; for they know not what they do" was his first utterance (Luke 23:34). His charity toward the soldiers who had nailed him to the cross, and now divided his clothing, was not deadened by his ordeal. Most of his apparel, a gratuity to the soldiers for fulfilling their military duty in the crucifixion process, held little value for the soldiers. But his inner garment or tunic, "without seam, woven from the top throughout," was contested (John 19:23). "Let us not rend it," one soldier was heard to say, "but cast lots for it, whose it shall be" (John 19:24).[8]

As lots were cast and the winner of the garment determined, Jewish leaders, "the same satanic souls who had orchestrated the calls for crucifixion now led the same chorus of voices in chanting a derisive hymn of hate and vengeance against [Jesus] who had been crucified."[9]

Joining in the abuse were the soldiers, who played a game of chance, and one of the thieves hanging on a cross near Jesus. Listening to the insults of the careless thief, who in his last hours was defaming the Son of God, was his accomplice. "Dost not thou fear God, seeing thou art in the same condemnation?" asked the penitent thief. "This man hath done nothing amiss" (Luke 23:40-41). He then said to Jesus, "Lord, remember me when thou comest into thy kingdom" (Luke 23:42). Jesus answered, "Verily I say unto thee, To day shalt thou be with me in paradise" (Luke 23:43).[10]

We assume his words, in contrast to the abusive words spoken near the cross, were appreciated by the women who

Via Dolorosa or Way of the Cross has fourteen stations that mark the traditional route Jesus followed from the judgment hall to Calvary.

The third and fourth Stations of the Cross along the Via Dolorosa.

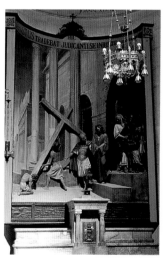

The Franciscan Chapel of Flagellation or Condemnation commemorates the site where Jesus was given the cross or crossbar to bear.

stood nearby listening to the derision—Mary, his mother, Mary the wife of Cleophas, Mary Magdalene, and Salome, the wife of Zebedee and mother of James and John. When Jesus saw his mother among the women listening to the unbridled mocking, he said, "Woman, behold thy son!" (John 19:26).[11] Turning to John the Beloved, who also

Golgotha or Place of the Skull, is believed by many to be the place where Jesus was hung on the cross between two malefactors. The crosses would have been placed at the bottom of the hill in a busy roadway, where scorners mocked the condemned. Today, it is the site of a busy bus station.

(opposite page) The small cupola on the Temple Mount is near where some archaeologists believe the Holy of Holies was located.

The Torah scrolls are kept behind scarlet curtains near the Western Wall. The curtains are a symbolic reminder of the veil of the temple.

stood near the cross, he said, "Behold thy mother! And from that hour that disciple took her unto his own home" (John 19:27).

At the ninth hour Jesus cried aloud, "Eli, Eli, lama sabachthani? that is to say, My God, my God, why hast thou forsaken me?" (Matthew 27:46). Again the Beloved Son knew anguish and pain—the Atonement.

Even in these hallowed moments, the jeers of the onlookers were not arrested. "This man calleth for Elias. . . . let us see whether Elias will come to save him" (Matthew 27:47, 49). As the irreverent looked for a heavenly manifestation of an ancient prophet, Jesus was heard to say, "I thirst" (John 19:28). In compassion, one man "ran, and took a spunge, and filled it with vinegar, and put it on a reed, and gave him to drink," but again Jesus would not partake (Matthew 27:48).

"It is finished . . . Father, into thy hands I commend my spirit" (John 19:30; Luke 23:46). And thus "he gave up the ghost," and Jesus of Nazareth, King of the Jews, was dead (Luke 23:46). Our Redeemer, our Savior, our Lord was crucified.

The heavens mourned, and darkness shrouded the skies over Jerusalem. Although for centuries the Jews had superstitiously viewed the obstruction of the sun as an "evil sign to the nations of the world," darkness at noon in Jerusalem on this day was different. Black skies and a tumultuous earthquake evoked fear and terror within those who still stood near the cross. Women "smote their breasts" and a centurion cried aloud, "Truly this was the Son of God," or as Luke writes, "Certainly this was a righteous man" (Matthew 27:54; Luke 23:47-48).

Even as the Holy City reeled in those dark hours, Jewish leaders were not penitent. They were conversing with Pilate, seeking to safeguard the sanctity of the

approaching Sabbath—the Day of the Lord. To them, it was imperative that the condemned men hanging on crosses at Golgotha be removed before Sabbath began.

Roman leaders had agreed with the Sanhedrin decades before to allow the removal of corpses from Golgotha before nightfall. Since the bodies could not be taken down from the crosses before death, the Jewish leaders were asking Pilate to command his soldiers to break the legs of the crucified to hurry the death process. If their legs were broken, the condemned would quickly die from respiratory failure and their bodies could then be taken from Golgotha before Sabbath began. Even though Pilate must have been concerned with the elements in turmoil and his subjects and soldiers in fright, he agreed to their request. Soldiers fulfilled Pilate's instructions and broke the legs of the thieves who hung on crosses on either side of Jesus, but when they discovered that Jesus was dead, his legs were not broken. (See John 19:33.) "But one of the soldiers with a spear pieced his side, and forthwith came there out blood and water" (John 19:34).

Gospel writers record that a disciple of Jesus—"a rich man of Arimathea, named Joseph"—approached Pilate towards evening, begging Pilate to grant his petition to take away the body of Jesus from Golgotha and bury his remains (Matthew 27:58). Joseph's request violated Jewish law, which decreed that Jesus did not have the right to an honorable burial.[12] However, Roman law allowed an honorable burial for prisoners convicted of political crimes. Since Jesus was executed for political reasons and not blasphemy before Pilate, according to Roman law he could receive an honorable burial. Pilate granted Joseph's petition.

Joseph retrieved Jesus' body from the cross, then he and others wrapped the body in a linen cloth and carried it from Golgotha to a nearby private tomb located in a garden.[13]

(See Matthew 27:59.) Joseph had "hewn out of a rock" an Herodian tomb that had two chambers—an outer chamber or anteroom used for wrapping the body, and an inner chamber used for burying it (Mark 15:46). The inner chamber had niches carved in the stone to receive the dead.

The body of Jesus was prepared for burial in a simple manner.[14] According to Jewish practice, the body was washed and then rubbed with oil and sprinkled with perfume. Nicodemus supplied "a mixture of myrrh and aloes, about an hundred pound weight" to anoint the body (John 19:39), which was then wrapped in grave clothes made of long strips of inexpensive linen called tachrichin wrappings or traveling-dress. Myrrh and aloe were packed between the strips of linen to lessen the stench of death. The wrappings, together with the powdered paste, produced a kind of "cocoon" around the body. The head was bound with a linen napkin, like a twisted turban, and the jaw held in place by a linen strip under the chin. According to the manner of the Jews, the neck and face were left uncovered. When the dressing was completed, it was said that the dead had been symbolically prepared for a journey into the eternities.

Jesus' body was placed in a niche in the burial chamber "wherein was never man yet laid" (John 19:41). A disk-shaped stone was then rolled edgeways in front of the entrance of the tomb to keep the body safe from intruders and wild animals. Joseph and Nicodemus then left the burial site, knowing that their actions had been kind, although hurried so as not to encroach on the Sabbath.

"Now the next day, that followed the day of the preparation," meaning the Jewish Sabbath, chief priests and Pharisees "came together to see Pilate" (Matthew 27:62). "Sir, we remember the deceiver said, while he was yet alive, After three days I will rise again," they told Pilate. "Command therefore that the sepulchre be made sure until

(opposite page) A round stone was used to block the entrance to the sepulchre.

Jesus lay in the burial chamber of the Garden Tomb for three days.

When Jesus died, darkness covered the land for three hours, from the sixth to the ninth hour, being from noon to 3:00 p.m.

the third day, lest his disciples come by night, and steal him away, and say unto the people, He is risen from the dead: so the last error shall be worse than the first" (Matthew 27:63-64).15 Pilate said, "Ye have a watch: go your way, make it as sure as ye can" (Matthew 27:66). So the Jewish leaders went their way and sealed the stone in front of the sepulchre, then set soldiers to guard the tomb of Jesus.

As dawn neared, the soldiers must have seen Mary Magdalene and another Mary coming "unto the sepulchre at the rising of the sun" (Mark 16:2). What was unusual about these women, and others who soon followed, was their determination to examine the wrappings of the dead and bring "sweet spices, that they might" anoint the body of Jesus (Mark 16:1). Instead of finding the body of Jesus, they, like the soldiers who guarded the tomb, saw an "angel of the Lord [who had] descended from heaven, and came and rolled back the stone from the door, and sat upon it. His countenance was like lightning, and his raiment white as snow" (Matthew 28:2-3). The reaction of the soldiers to the divine manifestation was to shake and become as "dead men" (Matthew 28:4).

To them the angel did not speak, but unto the women he said, "Fear not ye: for I know that ye seek Jesus, which was crucified. He is not here: for he is risen as he said. Come, see the place where the Lord lay" (Matthew 28:5-6).

After seeing the place, the women followed the angelic directive to "go quickly, and tell his disciples that he is risen from the dead" (Matthew 28:7). With fear, and yet with great joy, the women ran "to bring his disciples word" (Matthew 28:8). Although they described the empty tomb, their "words seemed to [most of the disciples] as idle tales, and they believed them not" (Luke 24:11). But Peter and John "ran unto the sepulchre; and stooping down, [they] beheld the linen clothes laid by themselves, and departed," knowing that they also had seen an empty tomb (Luke 24:12).

97

✤ Christian pilgrims worship inside many chapels within the Church of the Holy Sepulchre.

▶ A Christian pilgrim kisses the burial slab upon which many believe Jesus was laid.

▶ (opposite page) Dome of the Rock as seen through arches.

But there was one who did not depart from the Garden that day. "Mary stood without at the sepulchre weeping: and as she wept, she stooped down, and looked into the sepulchre" (John 20:11). She saw two angels sitting where the body of Jesus had been laid. The angels asked her, "Woman, why weepest thou?" (John 20:13). She answered, "Because they have taken away my Lord, and I know not where they have laid him" (John 20:13). And after she had "thus said, she turned herself back, and saw Jesus standing, and knew not that it was Jesus" (John 10:14).

"Woman, why weepest thou? whom seekest thou?" the Resurrected Lord asked Mary (John 20:15). Thinking him a gardener, Mary said, "Sir, if thou have borne him hence, tell me where thou hast laid him, and I will take him away" (John 20:15). Jesus then said, "Mary" (John 20:16). The familiar voice was recognized, and she replied, "Master" (John 20:16).

Jesus of Nazareth had overcome the grave. "We know not how it is done any more than we know how creation commenced or how Gods began to be. Suffice it to say, man is; and suffice it to say, he shall live again."[16]

I know that my Redeemer lives.
What comfort this sweet sentence gives!
He lives, he lives, who once was dead.
He lives, my ever-living Head.
He lives to bless me with his love.
He lives to plead for me above.
He lives my hungry soul to feed.
He lives to bless in time of need.[17]

He blessed Cleopas and Luke on the road to Emmaus. (See Mark 16:12; Luke 24:13.) He blessed Peter, the apostles, and others at Jerusalem. (See Luke 24:34, 36; John 20:19.) He blessed the apostles at the Sea of Galilee and later five hundred men. (See John 21:1-23; 1 Corinthians 15:6.) And on the Mount of Olives, "he blessed them, he was parted from them, and carried up into heaven. And they worshipped him" (Luke 24:51-52). We worship him, also. We express our gratitude and love for the blessings we have received in knowing that Jesus overcame death and is the Resurrected Lord. To him be all glory and honor forever. He is our Redeemer and the Savior of us all. To this we humbly testify.

ENDNOTES

CHAPTER 1

1. Technically, Herod reigned from the Hula Valley above the Sea of Galilee, south to the borders of the Nabatian kingdom.

2. A small political faction known as the Herodians believed the dynasty of the Herods fulfilled a Messianic promise. Herodians contended that the reign of Herod brought security and wealth to the Jewish people.

3. The appearance of Gabriel to Zacharias is the first and only recorded angelic manifestation in the temple at Jerusalem.

4. Typically, Jewish women were betrothed between the ages of fourteen and sixteen, and Jewish men were betrothed between the ages of seventeen and eighteen. James E. Talmage, *Jesus the Christ.* Salt Lake City, UT: Deseret Book Company, 1983, p. 84.

5. The name *Joseph* means "Jehovah adds," and *Mary* means "rebellion" or "bitterness." Mary is equivalent to Mara, the name used by Naomi to describe her perceived misfortunes. (See Ruth 1:20.)

6. *Jesus* is the Hebrew equivalent of *Yehoshua* or *Jeshua.* In English the name is rendered *Joshua.* In its original form the name meant "help of Jehovah" or "Savior-Deliverer." The Hebrew form of *Messiah* is *mashiah,* meaning "anointed one." The Aramaic term for *Messiah* is also translated as "the anointed one," whereas the corresponding word in Greek is *Christos.* By combining the Hebrew with the Greek, the name *Jesus Christ* emerges.

7. Talmage, *Jesus the Christ*, p. 77.

8. John J. Rousseau and Rami Arav, *Jesus and His World.* Minneapolis, MN: Fortress Press, 1995, p. 39.

9. The registration was a census-taking method. Those who registered would not have paid taxes at the time of registration, but at a later date. Scholars contend that it was the Jewish Sanhedrin that determined the census in Palestine should be taken in ancient family lands.

10. The Gospel writer Luke indicates that Joseph sought room in a kataluma, meaning a guest room in a private house, not at the noisy khan.

11. Several caves on the hillside of Bethlehem were artificially enlarged, creating an upper chamber used as a dwelling and a lower chamber intended for animals. Shepherds used the lower chambers to shelter their flocks.

12. Kaari Ward, ed. *Jesus and His Times.* Pleasantville, NY: Reader's Digest, 1990, p. 22.

13. For forty days after the birth of a male infant and eighty days after the birth of a female offspring, Jewish mothers remained in seclusion, "which meant that [they were] not allowed to leave the house or to touch any holy object." Wolfgang E. Pax, *In the Footsteps of Jesus.* Jerusalem, Israel: Nateev Publishing, 1970, p. 37.

CHAPTER 2

1. The massacre of the innocents in Rama was foretold by Jeremiah as "Rahel weeping for her children" (Jeremiah 31:15).

2. Alfred Edersheim, *Sketches of Jewish Social Life.* Peabody, MA: Hendrickson Publishers, Inc., 1994, p. 117.

3. Talmage, *Jesus the Christ*, p. 106.

4. *Mishnah Bikkurim III*, as cited in Hayyim Schauss, *The Jewish Festivals: A Guide to Their History and Observance.* New York City, NY: Schocken Books, 1938, p. 178.

5. *Ibid.*, p. 177.

6. The first stop for caravans of pilgrims going from Jerusalem to Galilee was Beeroth, a Hebrew word meaning "wells." Beeroth is the traditional site where Mary and Joseph first missed Jesus.

7. Byron Merrill, "'Behold the Lamb of God:' The Savior's Use of Animals as Symbols," *Lord of the Gospels: The 1990 Sperry Symposium on the New Testament.* Bruce A. VanOrden and Brent L. Top, eds. Salt Lake City, UT: Deseret Book Company, 1991, p. 135.

8. The Gospel of Mark records Satan's wiles in a single verse, whereas the Gospels of Matthew and Luke present colorful detail, but exchange the second and third temptations.

CHAPTER 3

1. It should be noted that the word "repent" was the first recorded word of Jesus' ministry, just as it was the first word uttered by John as he preached in the wilderness. (See Matthew 3:1-2; 4:17.)

2. Nathanael, meaning "gift of God" or "God-given," was also known in the Gospels as Bartholomew, the son of Telamyon. Whether referring to the disciple as Nathanael or Bartholomew, it is the same man.

3. Talmage, *Jesus the Christ*, pp. 137-38.

4. The *Joseph Smith Translation* of John 2:4 reads, "Woman, what wilt thou have me to do for thee? that will I do; for mine hour is not yet come."

5. This was the first of thirty-six miracles attributed to Jesus in the Gospels. Scholar Donald Q. Cannon classified these miracles into six categories: 1) healings, 2) raising the dead, 3) casting out devils or evil spirits, 4) miracles of nature, 5) providing food, and 6) passing unseen. Donald Q. Cannon, "Miracles: Meridian and Modern," *Lord of the Gospels*, pp. 23-38.

6. F. F. Bruce, *New Testament History*. New York City, NY: Doubleday-Galilee, 1980, p. 153.

7. Alfred Edersheim, *The Temple: Its Ministry and Services as They Were at the Time of Christ.* Grand Rapids, MI: Wm. B. Eerdmans Publishing Company, 1994, p. 177.

8. Bruce M. Metzger and Roland E. Murphy, eds., *The New Oxford Annotated Bible: Containing the Old and New Testaments.* New York City, NY: Oxford University Press, 1991, p. 7.

9. Bruce R. McConkie, *The Mortal Messiah: From Bethlehem to Calvary.* 4 vols. Salt Lake City, UT: Deseret Book Company, 1981, 2:19.

10. *Ibid.*

CHAPTER 4

1. Matthew is also known as Levi, son of Alpheus. The name Matthew is of Hebrew derivation and means "gift of Jehovah." Matthew Levi was selected as one of the twelve apostles. He was also the author of the first evangelical Gospel.

2. Only two of the ten pools in Jerusalem are mentioned in the Gospels—the pool of Siloam and the pool of Bethesda.

3. The apostles are listed as a group four times in the New Testament—once by Matthew and Mark, and twice by Luke. Each listing has a different order of seniority, but each recognizes that Simon Peter was first and Judas Iscariot last. The writers also differ in name variation for the apostles. For example, Judas is referred to as Lebbeus Thaddeus by Matthew, Thaddeus by Mark, and Judas, the brother of James, by Luke. The writers place the twelve in three groups of four. The groupings do not designate native origin, for eleven of the twelve were from Galilee and only one was from Judaea—Judas. The groupings indicate a type of seniority but still leave the reader confused. However, the leader of each grouping is always mentioned first—Peter, Philip, and James of Alphaeus.

CHAPTER 5

1. Since the Aramaic word for dead is *matta,* meaning "town," it is likely Jesus replied, "Let the town bury the dead" or "let the town take care of your father." George M. Lamsa, *Gospel Light: Comments on the Teachings of Jesus from Aramaic and Unchanged Eastern Customs.* Philadelphia, PA: A. J. Holman Company, 1936, p. 62.

2. A woman with hemorrhages was unclean according to the Levitical law. Scholars claim that she approached Jesus from behind, so as not to defile him. (See Mark 5:27.)

3. McConkie, *Mortal Messiah,* 2:335.

4. Cunningham Geikie, *The Life and Words of Christ.* NY: Columbia, 1891, p. 520, as cited in McConkie, *Mortal Messiah,* 2:382-83.

5. The inhabitants of Tyre and Sidon reveled in the pagan worship of Ashtoreth and Baal. Ashtoreth was revered as a goddess of sensual love and as a sacred prostitute. Baal, meaning "lord" or "master," was worshiped as the most prominent pagan god of the Asiatics. To these imaginary gods residents of Tyre and Sidon offered gifts and sacrifices, even child sacrifices, to appease their shifting whims.

6. The traditional site of the transfiguration is a dome-like mountain in the Jezreel Valley known as Mount Tabor, meaning "mountain height." The mountain creates a natural corner or division between the ancient lands of Naphtali, Issachar, and Zebulon. It ascends 1,843 feet above sea level and is located six miles east of Nazareth. Scholars do not accept the traditional site as the correct location. They document a fortified city atop the Mount Tabor summit during the days of Jesus, which suggests to them that this mount was not suitable. They reason that the snow-capped Mount Hermon, the highest peak in Palestine, was the site. With confidence they point to the scriptural passage in Matthew, which states, "high mountain" (Matthew 17:1).

7. The cloud was reminiscent of an earlier cloud that had rested upon the tabernacle of Moses and a foreshadowing of a cloud that would cover Jesus as he ascended to heaven. (See Numbers 9:15-22, 11:25; Exodus 33:9-11; Acts 1:9.) Bruce R. McConkie, *Doctrinal New Testament Commentary: The Gospels.* Salt Lake City, UT: Bookcraft, 1988, p. 403.

CHAPTER 6

1. The Sea of Galilee has a variety of types and sizes of fish that date back to the time of Jesus. Its population of edible fish dating to antiquity are represented by three surviving groups—musht, barbel, and sardine. The tastiest is the musht fish Tilapia Galilea, nicknamed Saint Peter's fish. It acquired its nickname long after Peter obtained the tribute money. (See Matthew 17:27.)

2. Saint Jerome wrote of Roman soldiers inflicting this punishment on leaders of an insurrection led by Judas of Galilee.

3. Schauss, *Jewish Festivals,* p. 178.

4. Philo, an ancient philosopher residing in Alexandria, Egypt, wrote of an additional

purpose for the booths: "[They] were erected to bring evidence of misfortune at a time of good fortune, and a reminder of poverty to those who were wealthy." Schauss, *Jewish Festivals*, p. 200.

5. McConkie, *Mortal Messiah*, 3:134.

6. Talmage, *Jesus the Christ*, p. 377.

7. The woman was not married, but betrothed. Mosaic law dictated strangulation for acts of adultery committed by a married woman. For a betrothed woman, the punishment was stoning. (See Leviticus 20:10; Deuteronomy 22:22.)

8. Thomas or Didymus, a Greek word meaning "twin," has been ridiculed for initially doubting the resurrection of Jesus. In this scriptural passage, Thomas was courageously supportive of returning to Jerusalem.

CHAPTER 7

1. Lamsa, *Gospel Light*, p. 118.

2. The issue of where the multitude acquired the branches has produced two scholarly opinions. The first and most plausible is that the branches came from nearby Bethany, a small village known for its date trees. These trees produce large leaves called branches by the villagers. (See John 12:13; Revelations 7:9.) The second opinion is that the branches were carried from Jericho to Jerusalem for the Passover festivities.

3. This shout was the high point of the Hosanna Day celebrated during the Feast of Tabernacles. On that day worshipers waved palm branches and shouted their hosannas in remembrance of the exodus from Egypt and the wilderness homes of their ancestors. The adulation given Jesus is found in Psalm 118, and is referred to as the Hallelujah Psalm. "He is blessed who comes in Yaweh's name; From Yahweh's house we bless you!" (See Psalm 118:26.)

4. The parable of the king's son was the last parable spoken by Jesus in a public setting. Two other parables were shared with his apostles on the Mount of Olives: 1) the parable of the ten virgins (Matthew 25:1-12), and 2) the parable of the talents (Matthew 25:14-30).

5. Herodians were a political faction that wanted power and rule to remain in the family of the Herods.

6. The Sadducees not only lost a verbal round with Jesus, but lost much of their religious influence to the Pharisees. Their belief in strict observance of the Torah and their rejection of Judaic traditions was not popular with the people, nor were their denials of a resurrection.

7. The Pharisees thought of themselves as religious leaders of the Jews, and wore priestly attire traditionally worn only by priests. Jesus decried their actions as hypocritical—a pretense.

8. If Simon were still leprous, he wouldn't have been allowed to remain in Bethany or welcome guests to his home. To imagine a leper entertaining guests is absurd. But to think of Simon as one of many who rejoiced in the healing miracles of Jesus is plausible. (See Matthew 26:6.)

9. Talmage, *Jesus the Christ*, p. 476.

10. The worth of the silver Judas received for betraying Jesus is uncertain. Matthew refers to silver shekels, leading scholars to conclude that the amount equaled one hundred and twenty days' wages of a common laborer. In theological circles it is said that the silver was the price of a slave. At one time in Judaea this was true, but by 30-33 A.D. thirty pieces of silver would "only pay for a new tunic." Ward, *Jesus and His Times*, p. 250.

11. Christian theologians maintain that the room was furnished with a triclinium, a U-shaped low-lying table. Jewish scholars scoff at the notion. They claim that small, moveable tables were used by guests during the Passover Feast.

12. If slaves were in the upper room they would remain standing, symbolic of their continuous servitude.

13. The Mount of Olives, believed by Jews to have escaped the Great Flood, is described as a mile-long chain of hills with three prominent summits. (See Ezekiel 22:24.)

14. Scholar D. Kelly Ogden illuminated the appropriateness of the name Gethsemane: "Just as the blood (juice) of the grape or olive is pressed and crushed by the heavy stone in the press, so the heavy burden of the sins of the world that was Jesus' to carry would press the blood out of the body of this Anointed One." D. Kelly Ogden, *Where Jesus Walked: The Land and Culture of New Testament Times*. Salt Lake City, UT: Deseret Book, 1991, p. 143.

15. It is perhaps not without significance that this was the Jewish Seder, meaning "night of the watchers." On this night, Jewish men were to watch during the late hours for God to save his people.

16. McConkie, *Mortal Messiah*, 4:107, 124, 127.

17. *Ibid.*

CHAPTER 8

1. It is conceivable that Judas led the soldiers, first to the house where he and fellow apostles had eaten the Paschal Supper, and found the upper room empty. Judas then led the soldiers to Gethsemane, for he knew that "Jesus ofttimes resorted thither with his disciples" (John 18:2).

2. McConkie, *Mortal Messiah*, 4:130.

3. *Ibid.*, 4:143.

4. Normally, they met in council at the Hall of Gazith known as the Chamber of Hewn Stone, to judge judicial matters important to Judaea.

5. Talmage, *Jesus the Christ*, p. 179.

6. According to rabbinic law, keeping any type of fowl in Jerusalem was forbidden. To have a fowl or to touch a bird in the Holy City subjected a Jew to Levitical defilement.

7. Some scholars claim that the trial of Jesus was held in the Antonia fortress, rebuilt and enlarged by Herod the Great and named for Marcus Anthonius, Herod's early patron. Other scholars contend that the trial was held in Herod's palace.

8. The yard had once been the property of a potter and was believed to be the traditional site where Jeremiah prophesied the destruction of Jerusalem.

9. By tradition, the wife of Pontius Pilate was named Procla or Claudia Procula. She was inclined toward Judaism, and may have been a Gentile proselyte before becoming a Christian. In the Greek Orthodox church she is canonized.

10. According to the Mosaic law, to die by crucifixion was to be cursed, for "he that is hanged [upon a tree] is accursed of God" (Deuteronomy 21:23).

11. If the sagum had been placed on a soldier or a foreign king, it would have been a recognition or symbol of wealth and royalty.

12. "With this cry Judaism was, in the person of its representatives, guilty of denial of God, of blasphemy, of apostasy," the very crimes they claimed were committed by Jesus. Talmage, *Jesus the Christ*, p. 601.

CHAPTER 9

1. In Rome an interval, ordinarily two days, was permitted between the death sentence and the execution of a prisoner. This interval did not apply in Roman provinces.

2. Simon was from the Jewish colony of Cyrene in North Africa. Cyrene, established by Ptolemeus Lagi in about 300 B.C., was home to a number of Jews for generations.

3. The name may derive from the shape of the rock upon which the endbar of the cross stood or from its purpose—the Roman site of execution in Palestine.

4. Gall by itself, the juice from an opium poppy, was bitter and poisonous.

5. Ward, *Jesus and His Times*, p. 259.

6. Pax, *Footsteps of Jesus*, p. 196.

7. It is unlikely that the Roman procurator ordered the wooden block inscribed with Latin in the middle and Hebrew first. Most scholars believe that the language on the block appeared first in Latin, then Greek, and last Hebrew or Aramaic.

8. The soldiers used Roman dice made from bones. They shook the dice in their hands. When the contents were emptied on the ground, the soldier who had guessed the toss or lot won the inner garment.

9. McConkie, *Mortal Messiah*, 4:218-19.

10. According to Christian lore, the unpenitent thief was named Gastas and the penitent thief Dysmas.

11. The word "woman" seems impersonal today, but anciently to be called a woman was a mark of honor and respect. "To every son the mother ought to be preeminently the woman of women," was an old eastern saying. *The Life and Teachings of Jesus*. Salt Lake City, UT: Corporation of the President of The Church of Jesus Christ of Latter-day Saints, 1974, p. 40.

12. J. R. Dummelow, ed. *A Commentary on The Holy Bible*. New York City, NY: Macmillian Company, 1964, p. 719.

13. These compassionate acts of Joseph would distance him from his associates in the Sanhedrin and cause him to be ritually unclean for seven days. His actions may also have brought duress to his family, who may have anticipated being buried in the tomb. Rabbis forbid the burying of kin in the tomb of an executed criminal.

14. In antiquity, the dead were buried in costly garments. Such practice halted at the death of Rabban Gamaliel. Gamaliel requested to be buried in simple linen shrouds so that Jews for generations to come would say, "What was good enough for this aristocrat is good enough for us."

15. Their plea for Roman soldiers to guard the tomb was probably unnecessary. The chief priests had complete access to the services of temple guards and could easily have commanded guards to seal the tomb and make it secure. They also had the legal right to take a guard, meaning a small squad of Roman soldiers, to assist them.

16. McConkie, *Mortal Messiah*, 4:257.

17. Samuel Medley, "I Know that My Redeemer Lives," *Hymns of The Church of Jesus Christ of Latter-day Saints*. Salt Lake City, UT: The Church of Jesus Christ of Latter-day Saints, 1985, No. 136, verse 1.

BIBLIOGRAPHY

Ackroyd, P. R., A. R. C. Leaney, and J. W. Packer. *The Gospel According to Matthew*. London, England: Cambridge University Press, 1963.

Barrett, C. K. *The New Testament Background*. San Francisco, CA: Harper & Row, 1989.

Bennion, Lowell L. *The Church of Jesus Christ in Ancient Times*. Salt Lake City, UT: Deseret Sunday School Union, 1963.

Berrett, LaMar C. and D. Kelly Ogden. *Discovering the World of the Bible*. Provo, UT: Grandin Book Company, 1996.

Brown, Raymond E. *An Introduction to the New Testament*. NY: Doubleday, 1997.

Bruce, F. F. *New Testament History*. New York City, NY: Doubleday-Galilee, 1980.

Cartidge, D. R. and D. L. Dungan, eds. *Documents for the Study of the Gospels*. Minneapolis, MN: Fortress Press, 1994.

Charlesworth, J. H. *Jesus within Judaism*. NY: Doubleday, 1988.

Clark, J. Reuben, Jr. *Behold the Lamb of God*. Salt Lake City, UT: Deseret Book Company, 1962.

———. *Our Lord of The Gospels*. Salt Lake City, UT: Deseret Book Company, 1957.

Connolly, Peter. *A History of the Jewish People in the Time of Jesus from Herod the Great to Masada*. NY: Peter Bedrick Books, 1983.

Dummelow, J. R., ed. *A Commentary on The Holy Bible*. New York City, NY: Macmillan Company, 1964.

Edersheim, Alfred. *Jesus the Messiah: An Abridged Edition of the Life and Times of Jesus the Messiah*. Grand Rapids, MI: Wm. B. Eerdmans Publishing Company, 1976.

———. *Sketches of Jewish Social Life*. Peabody, MA: Hendrickson Publishers, Inc., 1994.

———. *The Life and Times of Jesus the Messiah*. Peabody, MA: Hendrickson Publishers, Inc., 1995.

———. *The Temple: Its Ministry and Services as They Were at the Time of Christ*. Grand Rapids, MI: Wm. B. Eerdmans Publishing Company, 1994.

Feldman, L. H. and G. Hata. *Josephus, the Bible and History*. Detroit, MI: Wayne State University Press, 1988.

Ford, Richard Q. *The Parables of Jesus: Recovering the Art of Listening*. Minneapolis, MN: Fortress Press, 1997.

Frank, Harry Thomas. *Discovering the Biblical World*. NY: Harper & Row, 1975.

Geike, Cunningham. *The Life and Words of Christ*. NY: Columbia, 1891.

Gower, Ralph. *The New Manners and Customs of Bible Times*. Chicago, IL: Moody Press, 1987.

Harpur, James. *The Miracles of Jesus*. London, England: Reader's Digest, 1997.

Heschel, Abraham Joshua. *The Sabbath: Its Meaning for Modern Man*. New York City, NY: Noonday Press, 1951.

Hite, Julie M. and Steven J. Hite, comp. *The New Testament: With the Joseph Smith Translation*. Orem, UT: The Veritas Group, 1996.

Hunter, A. M. *The Gospel According to John. The Cambridge Bible Commentary, New English Bible*. P. R. Ackroyd, A. R. C. Leaney, J. W. Packer, eds. NY: Cambridge University Press, 1965.

Hymns of The Church of Jesus Christ of Latter-day Saints. Salt Lake City, UT: The Church of Jesus Christ of Latter-day Saints, 1985.

Israel: Pictorial Guide. Herzlia, Israel: Palphot Ltd., n.d.

Jackson, Kent P. and Robert L. Millet, eds. *The Gospels*. Salt Lake City, UT: Deseret Book Company, 1986.

Jacobs, Louis. *The Book of Jewish Belief*. West Orange, NJ: Behrman House, Inc., 1984.

———. *The Book of Jewish Practice*. West Orange, NJ: Behrman House, Inc., 1987.

Jesus, the Son of Man. Copenhagen, Denmark: Scandinavia Publishing House, 1982.

Jospe, Raphael, "Sabbath, Sabbatical and Jubilee: Jewish, Ethical Perspective," *The Jubilee Challenge, Utopia or Possibility?* Hans Ucko, ed. Geneva, Switzerland: WCC Publications, 1997.

Lamsa, George M. *Gospel Light: Comments on the Teachings of Jesus from Aramaic and Unchanged Eastern Customs.* Philadelphia, PA: A. J. Holman Company, 1936.

The Life and Teachings of Jesus. Salt Lake City, UT: Corporation of the President of The Church of Jesus Christ of Latter-day Saints, 1974.

The Life and Teachings of Jesus and His Apostles. Salt Lake City, UT: The Church of Jesus Christ of Latter-day Saints, 1978.

Ludlow, Daniel H. *A Companion to your Study of the New Testament: The Four Gospels.* Salt Lake City, UT: Deseret Book Company, 1982.

Madsen, Truman G. *The Radiant Life.* Salt Lake City, UT: Bookcraft, 1994.

Matthews, Robert J. *Behold the Messiah.* Salt Lake City, UT: Bookcraft, 1994.

McConkie, Bruce R. *Doctrinal New Testament Commentary: The Gospels.* 2 vols. Salt Lake City, UT: Bookcraft, 1988.

———. *Mormon Doctrine.* Salt Lake City, UT: Bookcraft, Inc., 1979.

———. *The Mortal Messiah: From Bethlehem to Calvary.* 4 vols. Salt Lake City, UT: Deseret Book Company, 1981.

———. *The Promised Messiah: The First Coming of Christ.* Salt Lake City, UT: Deseret Book Company, 1978.

Metzger, Bruce M. *The Text of the New Testament: Its Transmission, Corruption, and Restoration.* NY: Oxford University Press, 1992.

——— and Roland E. Murphy, eds. *The New Oxford Annotated Bible: Containing the Old and New Testaments.* New York City, NY: Oxford University Press, 1991.

Murphy, Frederick J. *The Religious World of Jesus: An Introduction to Second Temple Palestinian Judaism.* Nashville, TN: Abingdon Press, 1991.

National Geographic Society. *Everyday Life in Bible Times.* National Geographic Society, 1967.

The New Testament of the New Jerusalem Bible. New York City, NY: Doubleday, 1986.

Ogden, D. Kelly. *Where Jesus Walked: The Land and Culture of New Testament Times.* Salt Lake City, UT: Deseret Book, 1991.

Pax, Wolfgang E. *In the Footsteps of Jesus.* Jerusalem, Israel: Nateev Publishing, 1970.

Rhymer, Joseph. *The Illustrated Life of Jesus Christ.* London, England: Bloomsbury Publishing Limited, 1991.

Roberts, B. H. *Outlines of Ecclesiastical History.* Salt Lake City, UT: Deseret News, 1902.

Rousseau, John J. and Rami Arav. *Jesus and His World.* Minneapolis, MN: Fortress Press, 1995.

Schauss, Hayyim. *The Jewish Festivals: A Guide to their History and Observance.* New York City, NY: Schocken Books, 1938.

Smith, Joseph, Junior. *Inspired Version, The Holy Scriptures Containing the Old and New Testaments, an Inspired Revision of the Authorized Version.* Independence, MO: Herald Publishing House, 1944.

Smith, William. *The New Smith's Bible Dictionary.* Reuel G. Lemmons, ed. Garden City, NY: Doubleday & Company, 1966.

Talmage, James E. *Jesus the Christ.* Salt Lake City, UT: Deseret Book Company, 1983.

Tinsley, E. J. *The Gospel According to Luke. The Cambridge Bible Commentary, New English Bible.* P. R. Ackroyd, A. R. C. Leaney, J. W. Packer, eds. NY: Cambridge University Press, 1965.

Van Orden, Bruce A. and Brent L. Top. *The Lord of the Gospels: The 1990 Sperry Symposium on the New Testament.* Salt Lake City, UT: Deseret Book Company, 1991.

Wagenknecht, Edward. *The Story of Jesus in the World's Literature.* NY: Creative Age Press, Inc., 1946.

Ward, Kaari, ed. *Jesus and His Times.* Pleasantville, NY: Reader's Digest, 1990.